"dear Paradise"

STORIES OF BALMORAL
AND ROYAL DEESIDE

Richard and Richard
McDERMOTT

BETFORD PUBLICATIONS

'dear Paradise' — Stories of Balmoral and Royal Deeside

Also by Richard and Richard McDermott
The Standing Windmills of West Sussex
The Standing Windmills of East Sussex

Once again for
OLIVE and SUE
with love

Richard McDermott (Publicity) Limited
31 Windsor Road, Worthing, West Sussex, BN11 2LZ, England

First edition 1979

Photoset and printed in England by Flexiprint Ltd, Worthing, Sussex

ISBN 0 906396 02 6

ACKNOWLEDGEMENTS

We are indebted to Her Majesty Queen Elizabeth II for the loan of her colour transparency of Balmoral Castle, and for allowing us to use and reproduce this as the cover for our book.

We are also grateful to Her Majesty for permission to reproduce two water colour paintings from the Royal Collection: Carl Haag's 'Picnic' (page 9), and J. W. Carmichael's 'Royal George' (page 43), as well as the engraving of Allt na Giuthasnach (page 17).

Our thanks are also due to Colonel W. G. McHardy, MVO, the former Factor at Balmoral, for his help and assistance; and to the members of Her Majesty's staff at Buckingham Palace, and Sandringham; and to the staff at the Royal Library, Windsor, and the Lord Chamberlain's Office, London; all of whom dealt with our enquiries so promptly.

The colour photographs of The Queen and Prince Philip, and the Royal Family, taken by Patrick Lichfield, are reproduced by courtesy of Camera Press Limited.

Monty Fresco's photograph of Prince Charles at Balmoral is reproduced by permission of Associated Newspapers Limited.

The photographs reproduced on pages 23, 27, and 61 are from the Radio Times Hulton Picture Library; the Royal Wedding picture on page 59 is by courtesy of Popperfoto; whilst the photograph on page 64 is reproduced by permission of Syndication International.

We are indebted to the Grampian Regional Council, Department of Leisure, Recreation, and Tourism for the use of photographs of Craithie Kirk (page 21), and Braemar Castle (page 39), and in particular thank Miss Ailsa Clubb, for her help.

The engravings of Aberdeen (page 15), and Balmoral (page 50), have been taken from our own collection.

To the best of our knowledge all facts are as stated, and although not listed, are taken from published or authenticated sources. Where necessary, however, certain statements in the text have been amplified by footnotes. We have also endeavoured to be as correct as possible in the spelling of place names, especially those with a Gaelic flavour, but if we have erred we offer our apologies and trust to be forgiven.

Worthing 1979   Richard and Richard McDermott

WHICH WAY TO PARADISE?

'*Think what is now,*
And what hath been.'
—SIR WALTER SCOTT (1771-1832)

Although many roads lead from Aberdeen to Balmoral, as far as Queen Victoria was concerned there was only ever *one* way to approach her Deeside paradise, and that was to leave the granite City at the western end of Union Street and retrace the route taken with her 'dear Albert' on that first happy occasion in 1848. This, nowadays, is basically the main A93 motor road.

Prince Philip, on the other hand, is said to much prefer approaching Balmoral along the upper road, the B974, which runs through Echt and Tarland, once the ancient sheepfold of Mar in the Howe of Cromar, and the headquarters (in days gone by) of smugglers engaged in the distribution of illicit whisky. To-day however, Tarland, a quiet country village, is best known as the hub of the famous 8500 acre MacRobert Trust, whose splendid Highland cattle (one of four pedigree herds) can be seen grazing on the fields of this fertile estate.

Of course, there *are* other ways of reaching Balmoral; along the Lower Deeside road for example — the B943, which will take the traveller within easy reach of the Banchory-Devenick kirkyard where, once upon a time, an unchristened child wandered as a *taran* among the gravestones crying 'Nameless! Nameless!' until a local cleric gave the wee ghastie rest by baptising the infant's grave, giving it the name Godfrey (meaning God and Peace).

It is along this self-same road that one may also discover the Pool on the Dee where less than a hundred years ago an alleged water kelpie was sighted, and up along the Crynoch Burn is the Pot of Corbie Linn at the bottom of which — according to legend — a water goblin guards a fantastic treasure.

But first, one must reach Aberdeen.

In former days when the roads were so bad that long journeys were not undertaken lightly, the most sensible method of getting from London to Scotland was to go by sea. Indeed, it was in this manner that Queen Victoria and Prince Albert travelled when they made their first visit to Scotland in 1842. It was only after the royal couple had acquired Balmoral that they found it more convenient to use the new railway. Their first experience of this revolutionary mode of travel was in 1841, when they journeyed by rail from London to Windsor. They repeated the journey in 1842, although at the end of that trip it is recorded that Prince Albert took the Conductor on to one side and admonished him for travelling too fast.

Opposite:
PRINCE CHARLES.
A thirtieth birthday picture taken at Balmoral. The Prince is wearing his grandfather's kilt, and is supported by Harvey, his pet Labrador.

(Photo: Monty Fresco)

5

By their continued patronage however, Queen Victoria and Prince Albert did much to popularise rail travel and after Albert's death, and throughout her long reign, the Queen made great use of the railway both at home, and abroad. It has been estimated that in total time Queen Victoria spent seven years of her life in Scotland; by the same token, she travelled well over 100,000 miles by rail simply commuting between Osborne, London, and Balmoral. Despite this, the royal family never acquired their own rolling stock, but paid for their travel, and that of their entourage, and used the special compartments built for them by certain of the main line operators but which remained the property of the company.

In 1861, Doctor Baly, a royal physician, was crushed to death by the wheels of a railway carriage when he fell through the floor of his compartment in a derailment which occurred between Wimbledon and Malden. It was this disaster which bred within Queen Victoria a great dread of railway accidents. Over the years she became so concerned at the 'alarming and serious state of the railways' that she wrote to Mr. Gladstone from Balmoral in October 1873 suggesting that 'we should soon see a different state of things — if a Director (of the railway company) was bound to go with the trains.'(*)

The Queen certainly exercised great concern in the welfare of the drivers of her own locomotives, and insisted that her own rail travel was governed by a self-imposed set of rules. These required that a pilot engine running on the same track, but fifteen minutes ahead, preceded the Royal special at whose approach all goods trains came to a halt. The speed of her train was never to exceed 40 m.p.h. (she once had her special stopped because of undue agitation in the movement of her carriage), and every journey was meticulously planned well in advance and a recognised programme of stops laid down so that the Queen and her party would have an opportunity to partake of meals and attend to their personal comfort. Here it can be noted that Queen Victoria was the first railway traveller to enjoy the advantage of a lavatory en suite.

In 1899, the Princess Victoria of Prussia, second daughter and fifth child of the Crown Prince and Crown Princess Frederick, visited her grandmother and accompanied her to Balmoral. The 23 year-old Princess has left behind a description of the railway trip north which began when she, together with the Queen and her suite, left Windsor station at 8.15 on a very sultry June evening aboard a fourteen carriage 'special' provided by the London and North Western Railway. Later, after an obligatory 'refreshment' stop at Leamington, the Princess took herself off to the 'lovely soft bed' which had been prepared for her in the Queen's private sleeping compartment — a signal honour, and one only previously accorded to the Queen's daughters the Princesses Helen, Louise, and Beatrice.

But despite the fact that each of the carriages was fitted 'with electrical communication and all the most modern improvements', and that the singularly fine arrangements of the royal apartment had been designed to

---

* *The Royal Trains* **by C. Hamilton Ellis. Published by Routledge & Kegan Paul.**

provide every degree of comfort, it was not a particularly peaceful night. The heat became excessive, and although Queen Victoria (who was then in her 71st year) lay under only the lightest of covers, her arthritic joints were painful and she was in need of constant attention. An additional problem arose when the ice melted and it became necessary to bale out the ice-box. All in all, it must have been a trying experience for the reputedly gay and spontaneous young Princess and she, no doubt, must have welcomed the necessity of having to get up and get dressed and be ready to partake of breakfast which was ready and waiting when the train reached Perth.

At first, the railway line ran only as far as Montrose. But this was soon extended to Aberdeen, and that City then became a major railway centre and, by custom, the acknowledged gateway to Royal Deeside. It was also the official finishing point for the fabulous 19th century railway 'races' in which the incredible 90 ton expresses of the North Eastern Railway, with their 7ft. 1¼in. diameter wheels, often achieved speeds in excess of sixty miles an hour.

Aberdeen being the nearest town of any size or importance to Balmoral, it was inevitable that the merchants and shopkeepers of the City would be among those commissioned to supply commodities to the Royal Household. Those who were selected did not hide their light under a bushel, but soon made evident their special patronage by displaying the Royal Coat of Arms. Thus, even to-day, in Aberdeen and along Deeside it is possible to discover beautifully etched, engraved, carved, and painted armorial bearings discreetly preserved as witness of former service not only to Queen Victoria and Prince Albert, Edward VII and George V, but also to heads of state, and principals of now long vanished European monarchies.

Once quit of the built-up residential outskirts of Aberdeen, and having passed through Peterculter, or 'Cooter' as it is sometimes called, with its coloured statue of the Scottish freebooter and outlaw Rob Roy in the Leuchar Burn, the main A93 road continues westward to Balmoral by way of Banchory, Ballater, and Aboyne. For the most part it runs parallel with the river which springs up from the Wells of Dee on the great plateau above Braeriach in the Cairngorms, in the shadow of Ben Macdui, second highest mountain in Britain. Queen Victoria once climbed this mountain on pony back, and was rewarded with a view of the 'grandest, wild scenery imaginable'.

At the approach to Banchory, the B980, which branches to the right, leads to Torphins and Lumphanan where, on Cairnbeathie Farm, a commemorative cairn marks the spot where Macbeth is said to have been wounded. He fled to Perkhill, and it was there, on the 10th March, 1057, that he was set upon and killed by either Macduff, or Malcolm Canmore whose nickname in the language of the time meant 'Bighead'.

A secondary road, beyond Torphins, passes close to Learney, home of Lord Lyon King of Arms, the one principal Herald of Scotland who takes his name from the national escutcheon. It is an office of great antiquity, and is thought to date from the time of the Celtic kings, and since it is held directly from the sovereign and not the Earl Marshal, Lyon does, in fact, precede the English King of Arms although at the time of the Union, it was understood he would rank after Garter King at Arms.

It is within Learney House that the famous Brux Claymore is preserved. This great wide-bladed sword had been taken from the dead hand of Cameron of Brux by Mowatt of Abergeldie, the man who killed him. It was returned to Catherine, heiress of Brux, by Alasdair Forbes who sought out Mowatt, and slew him. In due time Catherine and Alasdair were married and Catherine fulfilled her promise to give herself to the man who restored into her hand her father's sword.

Eastward from Learney is the Hill of Fare (1545ft.) where, at the Battle of Corrichie in 1562, George Fourth Earl of Huntly died of a stroke on the field of battle. His son, Sir John Gordon, was captured and taken to Aberdeen where he was later beheaded by the Maiden, an early form of guillotine. Following the execution Huntly Castle in Strathbogie was occupied and looted, and Edward II's silken tent, captured at Bannock-burn and given to Sir Adam de Gordon by Bruce himself, was wantonly destroyed.

When Queen Victoria and Prince Albert first took up residence in the old castle at Balmoral, it was then almost cut off from the rest of the world. But for them this remote tranquility was its great attraction. They relished the privacy, and the opportunity of getting away from the pretentious arti-ficialities of Buckingham Palace and Windsor, and to live a life far removed from the protocol and pageantry with which they were surrounded — even at Osborne.

BENJAMIN DISRAELI

For the Queen's senior ministers however, the inaccessibility of Balmoral was a great trial, and even 'dear Mister Disraeli' unburdening himself in private, bemoaned the difficulties of maintaining the smooth government of the country some six hundred miles from its capital. Glad-stone too, experienced similar problems, and upon one occasion after journeying to Balmoral for an audience, he was kept waiting for several days before the Queen would deign to see him — and all, presumably, because the Prime Minister had previously annoyed the Queen by suggesting that she delay her journey to Balmoral for a few days in order that she might prorogue Parliament!

Early on, an attempt had been made to ease the difficulty of travel by extending the rail link from Aberdeen to Banchory. It took eight years to build this section of the line at an estimated cost of £95,009.19s.1d., and when completed in 1853, a final touch was added by installing the newly improved electric telegraph system in the station master's office. Although intended purely for the use of the Queen's senior advisers, willy-nilly the station master's office became the clearing house for the receipt and despatch of a great many official and highly confidential messages of national importance. It also burdened the station master with many extra duties and responsibilities, as when the news was received at Banchory that Sebastopol had fallen, the unfortunate railwayman was obliged to saddle up his horse and ride the thirty odd miles to Balmoral to deliver the message. But it was a vast improvement on the arrangements of the mid-

8

19th century when, during the Queen's very early occupation of Balmoral, her despatches had to be brought up from the railhead at Perth by way of Glenshee and Braemar — a strenuous, mind-boggling journey for the courier. The more so during the short, dark, rain-soaked days of the late autumn. However, by the time the poor railwayman arrived at the castle with his news of Sebastopol, most of the occupants — including the Queen, Prince Albert, and their houseguests Prince Frederick William of Prussia, and Lord Granville had retired for the night. But all were eventually awakened and gave vent to their jubilation with a sparkle of fire-works and bonfires, and by signalling for the hilltop beacons to be lit.

Banchory itself is now quite modern, although its origins are ancient. Set in terraced slopes, there is a long established industry concerned with the distillation of scent from home grown lavender and violets. The little town is also the acknowledged centre for a remarkable drink called Atholl Brose. Attached to this 'heavenly brew' — which is much esteemed as a sovereign remedy for the alleviation of fevers — is the legend of the Wild Man of the Highlands, a fearsome monster of a man who went around terrorising and robbing unwary travellers. Discovering the shallow pool at which the Wild Man drank, Sir William from Atholl emptied all the water from the hollow drinking stone and substituted a potent brew of whisky and honey. The Wild Man, when he returned and drank his fill, staggered back and fell into a deep stupor in which state he was effectively shackled by the inventive Sir William.

Following this exploit Sir William married Ada, daughter of Malise, and heiress of Tullibardine, thus founding the family which, in time, became the Dukes of Atholl whose coat of arms have, as one supporter, a Wild Man in heavy chains.

9

There are many versions of what is called Atholl Brose, but in each recipe the constant factor is oatmeal, always a staple Scots diet. In 1431, Alexander Stewart Earl of Mar, wandering the hills tired, wounded, and hungry after being defeated in battle by Donald Balloch of Inverlochy, was found and befriended by a young girl who gave him a small quantity of meal. The Earl, using his shoe as a bowl, mixed the meal with water and gave thanks with the impromptu rhyme:

> *Hunger is a cook right good.*
> *Woe to him that sneers at food.*
> *Oaten crowdie in my shoe,*
> *Sweetest meal I ever knew.*

Centuries later, Doctor Johnson expressed himself somewhat differently: 'Oatmeal,' he said, 'is a grain which, in England, is given to horses but in Scotland it supports the people.' This jibe brought forth the tart rejoinder, 'Aye, sir, that's true; but where else in the world would you find such magnificent horses? Or such grand people?'

A short distance from Banchory town centre is the famous Bridge of Feugh which spans the water at a point just below the confluence of the Dee and the Feugh. It is a favourite vantage point in the summer and autumn

> *Tae see the Feugh gang roarin' by*
> *An' watch the salmon louping high*

whilst across the bridge, the B9077 gives access to the A957 — the so-called 'Slug Road' which eventually reaches a height of 750 feet above sea level before dropping down into Stonehaven, the county town of Kincardineshire.

The bridge is also the starting point for the B974, the Cairn o' Mount road, along which Edward I marched toward Elgin. This motor road, established on an old drove road, climbs up through Glen Dye amid rugged and desolate scenery to achieve a maximum height of 1475 feet. It then descends steeply (1 in 5 at some points) by way of the 'Clatterin' Brig' to Fettercairn 'the chiefest fortress of all the Mearns'.

From Banchory the A93 continues to run parallel with the Dee past the pleasant scenery of Inchmarlo Woods to the bridge at Potarch, and then on to Kincardine O'Neil which, like Whitestone to the south of Banchory, was once a thriving staging point for Highlanders who drove large herds of cattle southwards for the seasonal 'trysts' with buyers from the Lowlands.

Much of the modern development which has taken place in Aboyne is due to the interest of Sir Cunliffe Brooks of Glentanar, although the association of the Gordon family goes back to the very beginnings when, in 1670, Charles Gordon, fourth son of the 2nd Marquess of Huntly, being granted a charter to create a burgh of Barony established the original Charleston of Aboyne. Thus it is always the Chief of the Clan Gordon who is traditionally piped on to the wide flat Green of Charleston to open the Aboyne Games.

10

In 1880, Aboyne Castle, which had undergone many changes over the years — including the building of a mansion house, was re-styled by Sir Cunliffe Brooks, and it was whilst staying as a guest with Sir Cunliffe that Lillie Langtry, in the company of General Lord Strathnairn and Lady Erroll, drove over to Balmoral whilst Queen Victoria was in residence and signed the visitor's book. When the Queen was shown the entry, she expressed regret at not having seen this most famous of all her eldest son's many mistresses.

LILLIE LANGTRY

Originally, the Aberdeen shipbuilding industry had centred upon the supply of wooden ships to local fishermen, but by the 17th century the City had become the leading shipbuilding port in Scotland; a prosperity which owed much to the abundance of oak and fir which grew along the Dee, particularly in the rich forest of Glen Tanar, to the south of Aboyne. Another factor was the proximity of the water which provided a cheap method of transporting the timber, especially when the Tanar and Dee came into flood after the winter snows had melted. The logs were simply tumbled on to the Dee's 'broad rushing tide' and rafted to Aberdeen by teams of lumberjacks. Having made the trip, the men would then walk the forty miles back to Glen Tanar, pick up another batch of logs and repeat the performance, for as long as the water was right. Small wonder that when Alex Hall built what was probably the world's first ever true clipper ship in the Footdee district of Aberdeen, he named her *Glen Tanar*.

Just how the term 'clipper' came into use is a matter for conjecture, although it has been suggested it came about through the capture of the French built *Cleopatra cum Antonio* by the British. Acknowledged to have been the swiftest, sweetest, moving craft ever to have been taken, she was converted into a corvette by the Royal Navy and re-christened *Clipatra*, and it is this name which the seamen of the time corrupted into 'clipper'.

Built and launched in six weeks at a cost of £5377, the great feature of the *Glen Tanar* was her sharply designed knife-edged bow which allowed the vessel to 'clip' through the water easily and cleanly, in contrast to the dogged progress of ships who favoured the more usual apple-cheeked bow. But perhaps the most famous of Aberdeen's ships was the graceful little tea-clipper *Thermopylae* constructed by Walter Hood from designs by Bernard Waymouth. Launched in 1868 she made her maiden voyage from the Lizard to Newcastle in Australia, and later completed the trip from Foochow, in China, to London in seventy-nine days. Only one ship ever bettered this time, and that was the Clyde-built *Cutty Sark* who, in 1887-8, did the journey in seventy-one days.

The Aberdeen White Star Company, whose fleet included the *Thermopylae*, were noted for their smartly painted figureheads, and one such which depicted Prince Albert in Highland dress adorned the Aberdeen-built *Abergeldie*. Unfortunately, the *Abergeldie* struck a reef off the Gaspar Straits three years after being launched, and sank. If there are mermaids in those waters they must puzzle over this quaintly kilted effigy whose fixed gaze has sought these long years to penetrate the underwater gloom of their arcanum world.

11

2

STEEP FROWNING GLORIES

'He who first met the Highlands swirling blue,
Will love each peak that shows a kindred hue;
Hail each crag a friend's familiar face,
And clasp the mountain in his mind's embrace.'

—BYRON (1788-1824)

 Westward from Aboyne spreads the wildly open and heather-clad aspect of the Muir of Dinnet, now a National Nature Reserve. It is an area of outstanding beauty, which, during August, becomes a far reaching spread of vivid purple. Beyond is the clachan of Dinnet, the acknowledged eastern boundary of the Deeside Highlands. Of the many lakes which abound in this area it has always been said that two of the smaller of the islands on Loch Kinord are linked by a causeway, now lost beneath the risen water. Over on the western side of this same Loch is the Burn of Vat, a rock strewn gully that becomes a swirling, fearsome mass of water in time of flood.

Further along, but on the other side of the Dee and almost opposite Cambus O'May — 'the Crook on the Plain' — is Ballaterach and the celebrated chalybeate wells of Pannanich, first exploited by Francis Farquharson of Monaltrie.

Returning home after exile, the Jacobite Colonel, who had been captured at Culloden, was told of an old woman who, 'guided by dreams', had cured herself of either the King's Evil or consumption (there are differing stories) by bathing in the blue-scummed waters of the bog. Sensing the value of such a 'cure', the businesslike Colonel located the wells, had them cleaned and covered, and then set about spreading the word of the old woman's restoration to normal health.

The result exceeded all expectations. The wells became fashionable, and to accommodate the people who, from 1760 onwards, flocked into the area to take the waters, the village of Ballater, and the hamlet of Pannanich came into being. For the richer patron the Colonel built Pannanich Lodge, a spa hotel at Cobbletown. Later in the following century when the popularity of the wells was on the decline, Queen Victoria visited the Lodge on one of her 'excursions'. She described it as a 'curious little inn', and having partaken of the waters pronounced them to be 'strongly impregnated with iron'. It was here too, that John Brown who became the Queen's Highland Servant, first found employment before Sir Robert Gordon took him on to his staff at Balmoral.

In 1795, the young Byron, who had been born with a lame foot, was sent to Ballaterach as a sickly seven-year-old to recover from a bout of scarlet fever. An unflattering miniature, painted at that time, shows him as a long faced, melancholy looking boy with large wild eyes, a big nose, protruding ears, a pursed cupid's bow mouth, sloping shoulders, and cropped hair. He stayed with John Robertson and his wife at the farm at Ballaterach, took the waters, and consumed vast quantities of goat's whey. The impressions stored up by the young Byron as he 'roved a young Highlander' burgeoned in his later poetry; as did his regard for Mary, the Robertson's 13-year-old daughter whom he immortalised in verse:

> '. . . as rude as the rocks, where my infancy grew,
> No feeling, save one, to my bosum was dear;
> Need I say, my sweet Mary, 'twas centred on you?'

Byron's constantly recurring love of the Highlands was undoubtedly due to the fact that the Gordons were his maternal ancestors. His mother was Catherine Gordon of Gight, whose castle in the Braes of Gight between Fyvie and Methlick boasted a ghostly piper whose eerie lament could be heard as he wandered mournfully up and down the dark passages.

Gight also possessed a centuries old heronry, about which the 13th century rhyming prophet Thomas of Ercildoune ('Thomas the Rhymer') had predicted:

> When the heron leaves the tree
> The lairds o' Gight sall landless be

LORD BYRON
Sketch based on the portrait by Thomas Phillips in the National Gallery.

Byron's father, 'Mad' Captain John Byron, son of Admiral 'Foulweather' Jack Byron, and grandson of the 5th and 'Wicked' Lord Byron, contracted two marriages — both of which were for money. His first wife, whom he seduced, was the wealthy Lady Carmarthen. After her divorce, they married and went to live in France, but of their three children only one survived: Byron's half-sister Augusta, who was destined to become a central figure in the poet's later life. When his wife died, all income ceased and so the penniless Captain was obliged to return to England to seek out a new wife. As far as he was concerned it did not matter who, or what she was, just as long as she had money. He found what he was looking for in Bath in the shape of Catherine Gordon.

Shortly after their marriage in 1785, the herons suddenly foresook the grounds of Gight Castle and established a new, and thriving colony on the other side of the River Ythan. Within two years Thomas the Rhymer's prediction was fulfilled to the letter: John, having recklessly squandered away her fortune, the luckless Catherine was obliged to sell Gight Castle to pay off her husband's debts.

To avoid the bailiffs the couple fled to the Continent, and whilst in Paris Catherine discovered she was pregnant. Determined that her child should be born in England she returned home, and at 16 Holles Street, Marylebone, on the 22nd of January, 1788, was duly delivered of a son. By the end of that year however, Catherine had had enough, especially as Captain John could not trouble to present himself at his son's christening. She did what countless other wives had done before her. Taking her infant son with her, she went home to mother, settling in lodgings in Queen Street, Aberdeen. But the Captain followed, and he too took lodgings in Queen

13

Street, Aberdeen, but at the opposite end from his wife.

In this strained manner, and for two years, this ill-matched couple eked out a precarious living on the small interest which Catherine derived from the money left over from the sale of Gight. Then suddenly, Captain John decamped to France, carrying with him every bit of money and all the valuable items he could lay his hands upon. He subsequently died in Valenciennes in 1791.

In 1798 the 'Wicked' Lord Byron died, and Byron, who had become heir presumptive when the 5th Lord's elder grandson had died in Corsica in 1783, succeeded to the title of Baron Byron of Rochdale. Within two months of the event, Byron's mother had sold up all her effects in Aberdeen, and she came south again taking up residence, with her son, in Newstead Abbey, the decaying family home in Nottinghamshire. Byron never again set foot in Scotland, and the house in Queen Street, Aberdeen, where he had resided with his mother, was eventually pulled down to make way for the new extension to Marischal College.

When the railway link between Aberdeen and Banchory was completed in 1853, the Deeside Extension Railway Company was formed to promote an ambitious plan to extend the line to Braemar. In reality, the new company was merely an off-shoot of the original Deeside Railway, although the two companies were kept separate. Each issued shares, each issued dividends, although it was always said that those declared by the Deeside Railway were better than those of the Extension.

From Banchory the new track branched out in a great loop connecting Glassel, Torphins, Lumphanan, Dess and Aboyne. From there it continued to Dinnet, and on to Cambus O'May. Although re-assuring reports were issued claiming the building was going ahead as planned, progress was slow; in fact, it was so painfully slow that people began to believe that 'behind the scenes' construction was being deliberately discouraged. Who can now say if this was so? All that is known is that it took fourteen years to lay twentyfour miles of railway line — a work schedule that certainly bears little relationship to the speed and enthusiasm with which new railway systems were, at that time, being built across the changing face of Britain.

Eventually, the Deeside Extension arrived at Ballater, but there, after establishing what in time became the most 'Royal' of all railway stations, the project ceased. At first, the widowed Queen refused to use the station, and still insisted on driving to Balmoral from Aboyne, using a hired carriage. However, she did eventually capitulate, and Ballater became the accepted 'local' station for the Royal family at Balmoral. Part of the projected trackway, known locally as 'The Old Line', has been made into a footpath and this provides a charming walk through the gorge to a point where the Gairn and the Dee meet.

Ballater and Braemar are the recommended approaches to Lochnagar, or 'The Goat's Lake'. From Ballater it is some 13½ miles to the summit, some of which can be done by car. The route starts on the south side of the Dee, which is crossed by Ballater Bridge, 'The Royal Bridge', opened by Queen Victoria in 1885. It continues on and over the Bridge of Muick, one

14

of those old bridges which were traditionally designed with a high centre arch in order that travellers would know when they were on the bridge, and when they were off. A little further on it passes Birkhall, the 'house in the glen', now part of the Balmoral estate. It was built in 1715 by Charles Gordon after Abergeldie Castle had been taken over by General Mackay, as a garrison. Originally it was called Stiren, and its 6500 acres were included in the Abergeldie estate. It was purchased from the Gordon family as a home for Albert Prince of Wales, but in the event his occupancy was brief and he only lived in the house during 1862, the year before he was married. Upon the occasion of his marriage the tenants of the estate raised a commemorative cairn on Creag Bheag, one of the smaller of the Coyles of Muick, which stand between the Mill of Sterin and the Falls of Muick. When the cairn fell into disrepair, Queen Victoria caused a second to be raised on the top of the highest of the Coyles.

Since Charles Gordon first set his marker stone above the entrance over two hundred and sixty years ago, Birkhall has suffered little alteration. In 1885 the Prince of Wales sold the small Queen Anne house back to his mother, after which it became the the home of Edward Prince of Wales (Edward VIII), the Duke of York (George VI), and Queen Elizabeth the Queen Mother. Our present Queen also knows Birkhall very well indeed, for it was here that she spent much of her childhood, and part of her honeymoon.

Beyond, the road winds into Glen Muick with its 40ft. cascade, and ends at the picnic area adjacent to the Mountain Rescue Post. From here on, the journey to the top of Lochnagar must be completed on foot. Away in the distance is the great depression of Loch Muick, said to be an area much favoured by Prince Charles. It certainly fascinated Queen Victoria. 'So wild, so grand', she wrote, 'real severe Highland scenery'. Therefore nobody was really surprised when, in 1849, shortly after the Queen and

15

Prince Albert had leased Balmoral, the Royal couple took over a cottage in these wilds. It consisted of three rooms and a detached kitchen, and had been converted by Captain Gordon from two granite shiels — formerly used by ghillies — which had shared a sod roof, and a single window. After the royal purchase the property was much improved by the addition of public rooms, and bedrooms. But although elevated to the dignity of a Lodge, and officially named Allt-na-Giuthasach[1] (Fir Tree Burn), more often than not, the Royal couple and their growing family referred to it by its former name: 'The Hut'. It became a favourite starting point for their wanderings on Lochnagar and 'expeditions' made into the more remote regions of these High lands.

The trackway to the summit of Lochnagar runs behind, and above Allt-na-Giuthasach, then crosses a small bridge beyond which it is possible to discern the outline remains of the foundations of an 18th century smuggler's hut; one of the old 'black bothys'. Climbing higher, the Little Pap and Cuidhe Crom become visible; higher still, and one discerns the steeply zig-zagging pathway known as 'The Ladder'.

Although 'The Ladder' is a fairly steep climb, the trackway at the top (which passes close to the edge of the northern precipice) provides easy access to Cac Carn Beag. Then, surrounded by the majestic glories of dark Lochnagar, and revelling in the glow of self-achievement, the climber can stand before the indicator panel and tick off the well known landmarks that are open to the view.

When Prince Albert died, and one must remember that Queen Victoria lost both her husband and her mother all within one tragic twelve-month period, the Queen felt she could never again sleep in 'The Hut'. But her feeling for the wild beauty was so great, and her need for some sort of retreat so necessary, she commissioned the building of a new house. The neat, two-storeyed structure, erected at the upper end of Loch Muick on a site where Prince Albert had always wanted to build, was named Glassalt Shiel.[2] Here, on the 1st of October, 1868, after nineteen people (including the lone policeman who did duty outside) had gone through the ceremonies of fire kindling, or house warming, the Queen retired. When she was alone she confided to her diary:

> *'It is far better to have built a totally new home; but then the thought struck me that this was the first Widow's House, not built by him or hallowed by his memory. But I am sure his blessing does rest upon it, and those who live in it.'*

Two years after this entry was made, the Marquis of Lorne, the Duke of Argyll's heir, went walking from Glassalt Shiel in the company of Queen Victoria's fourth daughter, the Princess Louise. Whilst on that walk the Marquis proposed to the Princess, and was accepted. They were married

---

1. **The spelling which we use here is as Queen Victoria's note heading. There are however, many variants: e.g. current OS.** *Allt-na-guibhsaich.*

2. **Again Queen Victoria's spelling. Present day:** *Glas-allt-shiel.*

16

ALLT NA GIUTHASACH. This illustration is taken from Her Majesty's Patterns of Writing Paper, held in the Royal Library, Windsor Castle.

on the 21st of March, 1871, the Princess being the only one of Queen Victoria's children to marry into Scotland.

Less arduous than the ascent of Lochnagar, but none the less rewarding, is the climb to the top of Craigendarroch (the 'Hill of the Oaks'), which stands 1300 feet above sea level on the north bank of the Dee. However, because Ballater's own elevation is 658 feet, the bulk of Craigendarroch rising above the village is correspondingly reduced. But despite this, and the fact that some of the pathway climb is a bit steep, the hill does serve as a fine natural grandstand from which to obtain a variety of delightful views of the surrounding countryside.

The B972 motoring road which skirts Craigendarroch, is the first stage of an interesting 26 mile jaunt over narrow roads and steep gradients to Tomintoul, in Banffshire. It crosses the single arched Bridge of Gairn, and then continues through the glen to Gairnsheil Lodge (which, as children, Queen Elizabeth and Princess Margaret always called 'Teapot Cottage'), where a right-hand turn is made on to a narrow road which leads, eventually, to Cock Bridge, considered the half-way point in the journey.

Here, the Cock Inn — properly the Allargue Hotel, which claims to be the highest permanently occupied hotel in Scotland — is easily recognised, as is Corgarff Castle. This 16th century tower house, originally built as a hunting seat, was the setting for a particularly savage chapter in the saga of the feuding Forbses and Gordons when, in 1571, Adam Gordon of Auchindoun attacked Corgarff and set it on fire. Twenty-eight people, including Margaret, the Laird's wife, were trapped within the castle, and all perished in the blaze.

After this terrible happening, the Earl of Mar partially restored the castle keep, and in 1645 it was briefly used by the Marquess of Montrose as a base during his battles against the Duke of Argyll. Forty-four years later, in 1689, the castle was again put to the torch. This time the fire-

17

raisers were the Jacobites who, in the 18th century occupied Corgarff and used it as an arms store until in March 1746 they fled at the approach of 400 Hanovarian troops under the command of Lord Ancrum. The tower was rebuilt at a later date, new wings were also added and the whole enclosed within a star-shaped loop-holed wall. It then became a garrison post, and remained in commission until 1831. The Castle is now in the care of the Ministry of Public Buildings and Works.

The Cock Bridge itself takes the A939 over the Don, and from there it starts its serpentine course over the mountains to Tomintoul. Beyond the bridge, at the border with Banffshire, the road narrows yet again as it follows a section of the Old Military Road to the Wells of Lecht, where a marker records the fact that the road was built in 1745 by the 33rd Regiment. This particular stretch of road reaches a height of 2114 feet above sea level. It is the second highest driving road in Scotland, and almost always the first in the country to become snowbound.

Some two miles from the Wells of Lecht the road widens and then, over some six miles, descends by way of Conglass Water into Tomintoul, at one time the 'dirtiest, poorest village in the Highlands'. But that was long ago at a time when the settlement was a rendezvous for outlaws, rogues, vagabonds, and cut-throats. Now however, our modern and hygienically pre-packed civilisations reach up even to these remote heights, and Tomintoul has become a splendid centre (with some good hotels) from which to explore the delights of the Valley of the Avon, pronounced A'an.

Basically, the community has developed from the settlement which grew up around the intersection of the then new Military Road from Lecht to Abernethy, and the two ancient trackways which led, the one to Tomnavoulin, the other to Ballindalloch, although the true foundation of the present village is attributable to Alexander 4th Duke of Gordon. Without denying the Duke's pioneering spirit however, it is reasonable to suppose his convictions might have been less certain, his support less generous, had it not been for the work of the Army paviours who, nearly a quarter of a century earlier, and in continuance of surveys carried out by General George Wade, hammered out the roads which brought ease of access to sequestered districts in such extreme heights as Tomintoul.

The clansmen, of course, hated the new roads, regarding them as a personal affront to their individual liberty, and as being of no possible use to anybody, except the Redcoats. But others, like the Duke, did not feel it was the world coming to an end. They had the sense to discern the inner truth of the rhyme which was then becoming popular:

> *Had you seen these places*
> *When the roads were yet unmade,*
> *You'd raise your hands to Heaven*
> *In praise of General Wade.*

Whilst posterity will always acknowledge achievements of great men in a correct and proper fashion, more often than not they are remembered by ordinary men and women for some simple happening; something apart, which captures and holds the imagination: Alfred and the cakes, for example, Bruce and the spider, James Watt and his kettle, Newton and his apple. So too is it with General Wade, a soldier who is best remembered for the roads he built.

In 1725, after pursuing a military career that had been distinguished without being spectacular, he was appointed to command the Army in Scotland. He was then 53 years of age, stout, inclined to bad temper and, in 1722, had been elected as the Member of Parliament for Bath. His prime objective, in Scotland, was to establish a more civilised system of Clan control, a task that was far from easy but one which he achieved in a manner both unique, and bloodless. He initiated a programme of road-building which went on over a period of ten successive years, and which aimed at creating a direct route between Blairgowrie in the south, and Inverness in the north. A second road system connected Fort George, built by Wade in 1726, with Fort William, founded by General Monk, and Fort Augustus (Kilcumin), built by Wade in 1730. Collectively, these three Forts in the Great Glen were known as 'The Chain'.

It has been estimated that the General was responsible for the laying down of more than 500 miles of road (most of which was 16 feet wide), over extremely remote and difficult terrain. He also built some 40 bridges and in all, created a system which opened up the High lands in a manner never before thought possible. Indeed, it is hard to believe that less than two hundred years ago these isolated areas of Scotland were as unknown to the people of the outside world as the Amazon forests, and that during the whole period of their long occupation of Britain not one Roman soldier ever set foot in these regions.

From Tomintoul, the A939 continues to the Bridge of Brown, and then still following parts of the Old Military Road, climbs over the high moors before descending into Grantown-on-Spey, thus completing the connection between Deeside and Speyside.

From Ballater there is another, and more adventurous route up to Tomintoul. This starts by following the B972 motor road to the junction of Gairnshiel Lodge, and then continues along the A939 toward Balmoral. A mile or so beyond the Lodge, a very minor, and unfenced road branches to the right and follows around the base of Cnoc Chalmac to Daldownie, crossing first the Duchrie Burn, and then the River Gairn. To the right is Brown Cow Hill, on the lower slopes of which is Corndavon shooting lodge. Eventually, this road peters out at Loch Builg near the ruins of Lochbuilg Lodge. From here 'where the antlered stag is free to rove at will', the journey is all on foot — a good, solid 10 mile hike following the remote track through the Builg Burn to Inchrory, and then up the Valley of the Avon, to Tomintoul. In 1860 Queen Victoria and Prince Albert, accompanied by experienced guides, did this trip in reverse.

3

'FRIEND MORE THAN SERVANT'

'The rank is but the guinea stamp;
The man's the gowd for a' that.
Ye see yon birkie ca'ad a lord
Wha' struts and stares, and a' that?
Tho' hundreds worship at his word,
He's but a coof for a' that.
For a' that, and all that:
The man of independent mind
He looks and laughs at a' that.

—ROBERT BURNS (1759-1796)

Standing over on the south side of the Dee some six miles from Ballater, at a point where the Geldie Burn enters the Dee, one could declare Abergeldie Castle to be romantically situated. But its position was not governed by surrounding beauty, but upon hard-headed, commonsense fact: it strategically controlled both the Geldie ford, and the old road which used to cross into Angus at this point. George Fenwell Robson, the 19th century artist, described it as 'one of those ancient country residences which indicate by their high and massive architecture, the turbulences of the times in which they were erected'.

The Castle was granted to the Gordon family by James the First in 1487, and it has remained in their possession ever since. Even when Queen Victoria and Prince Albert made it known they would like to buy Abergeldie, the Gordons preferred not to sell outright. Therefore, although Abergeldie adjoins Balmoral and is part of the estate, it is not royally owned but is held, by the Queen, on a long lease.

On the north side of the Dee, the pine and larched fringed scenery of the westward route from Ballater has been called 'gracious', 'serene', and 'charming', but during the months of August and September when the Queen is in residence at Balmoral, and on those Sundays when the Royal family attend Divine Service at Crathie kirk, about two miles distant, the traffic does tend to build up.

Between the road and the river, in the Crathie kirkyard, can be seen the roofless, ivy-clad ruins of the ancient pre-Reformation church one wing of which however, is reserved as a burial place for the Invercauld family. Last repaired in 1731, it remained in regular use until replaced by a new kirk, built in 1804 at a cost of £850. This was the small, white-washed church used by Queen Victoria and Prince Albert when they came to Balmoral. In those days the minister was the Rev. Archibald Anderson. He served the parish well for 26 years, and his collie dog greatly delighted the Queen with his habit of following his master into the pulpit and remaining there

20

until the sermon was preached. In 1873, this little church was graced by a two-light stained glass window; the gift of Queen Victoria and to the memory of Norman Macleod, who had preached his first sermon as Court Chaplain at Crathie, on the 29th of October, 1854.

By 1893 however, when Queen Victoria's habit of partaking Communion at Crathie had become well established, it was generally agreed that the time had come for a new church to be built; one which would be more suited to 'the peculiar needs of the parish'. And so, on the 24th April, 1893, demolition of the old church began, and during the time it took to make ready a temporary church, the parishioners continued their worship in the Iron Ballroom at Balmoral, placed at their disposal by the Queen.

Work on the new church progressed so well, that within a few short months it was possible for the foundation stone to be laid. This ceremony, which took place on the 11th September, 1893, was performed by Queen

Victoria, and after she had replied to the loyal address 'in a wonderfully distinct voice' three of her grandchildren came forward and annointed the stone with corn, oil, and wine.

The Church building fund, to which Queen Victoria donated the sum of £500, and the Farquharson family of Invercauld, a similar amount, was also doing well although it was still short of the £6000 considered necessary to complete the work in the manner planned. It was to make good this deficiency that the Princesses Louise and Beatrice proposed to raise money by setting up a Bazaar.

Accordingly, after months of preparation, the Bazaar took place in the Statue Park, Balmoral, on two days during the September of 1894. Numerous members of the Royal family contributed generously of their own handiwork, and this was on sale on the Balmoral stall run by the two Princesses. Although not specifically noted as such, Queen Victoria contributed several baskets which she had plaited herself. Sadly however, she recorded in her diary that at the end of the day a number remained unsold, and had to be auctioned off.

Built of white Inver granite, the new Crathie Church was erected to the design of Dr. A. Marshall Mackenzie, who also planned the modern wing of Marischal College, in Aberdeen. Cruciform in shape, it has a tiled roof, and a small spire atop of a massive tower, and occupies the same site as the old church right in the very centre of the parish. Since it was dedicated for worship in the presence of Queen Victoria and members of the Royal family on the 19th of June, 1895 however, there have been additions to the interior furnishings and memorials. The marvellous Communion Table and Screen, for example. This was a Royal gift in commemoration of King Edward VII. Among the many portrait busts are those of Princess Victoria, who married Frederick III, Emperor of Germany and King of Prussia, and was the mother of Kaiser Wilhelm II; King George the Fifth, and King George the Sixth, and one of Queen Victoria, which is set in the granite pillar immediately above the foundation stone.

Of the original furnishings, particular merit attaches to the pulpit, designed by Dr. Mackenzie, the architect. The Royal Household of Queen Victoria joined in the giving of this pulpit to the church. In its construction it incorporates no less than eighteen varieties of Scottish granite, and features a decorative moulding made up of choice marble pebbles collected by Princess Louise, and brought back from Iona.

Several notable members of Queen Victoria's staff are buried in the Old Crathie kirkyard, including her 'devoted personal servant' John Brown. A crowd of over 500 people attended his funeral, which took place on the 5th of April, 1883, after which it was discovered that vandals had removed every one of the labels which had been attached to the various wreaths sent by people of rank. Brown's headstone, a sturdy pedimented slab of Aberdeen granite buttressed with an ornamental iron railing* to protect

*   *This has long disappeared.*

JOHN BROWN,
Queen
Victoria's
Highland
Servant.

the grave, was ordered by the Queen herself. She also composed the inscription:

This stone is erected
in affectionate
and grateful remembrance of

JOHN BROWN

The devoted and faithful
personal attendant
and beloved friend of

QUEEN VICTORIA

in whose services he had been
for 34 years

To this was added the following lines, suggested by Lord Tennyson:

That friend on whose fidelity you count;
That friend given you
By circumstances over which you have no control,
Is God's own gift.

Public interest was so great, that after the headstone had been erected a regular coach service was inaugurated to bring sightseers to the grave. Their presence, and their numbers, caused Lord Bridport to suggest to the minister's wife that she would do well to levy a charge of a shilling a head. There had been so much speculation in the press of the time and by word of mouth as to the true nature of the relationship between Queen Victoria and John Brown, that it is a great pity his own private diaries were impounded and burned, with the Queen's full approval, by Sir Henry Ponsonby, her Private Secretary and Equerry. Had they survived, they might have shed some welcome light on this rather dark subject.

John Brown, the second child in a large family, was born on the 8th of December, 1826 in the little village of Crathienard, just across the Dee from the spot where he now lies buried. His father was a farmer, and his mother, who came from Aberarder, was the daughter of the village blacksmith. Two of John's brothers died in childhood, another in his teens. His sister, who he idolised, died when she was fourteen. Beyond that, the ancestry of the Brown family is confused and remote, and this is due in no small measure to Queen Victoria who, in order to give him status in the eyes of the other servants in the Royal household, endeavoured to create a pedigree.

To do this, she sought the aid of Dr. Andrew Robertson, who was then the only doctor within a fifty mile radius of Balmoral, and who had brought John Brown into the world. Unfortunately, the good doctor was a sycophant of the first water, and much of the 'tree' which he prepared, and the 'links' he forged between John Brown and families such as the Farquharsons of Inverary, were pure nonsense; from beginning to end the pedigree was written specifically to please the Queen, and in this the doctor was successful. The work was widely circulated amongst the Royal family, and members of the Queen's household, and to give Brown further lustre, she ensured his portrait was included in a gallery of 'Highlanders of Scotland' (compiled by Kenneth Mackeay of the Scottish Royal Academy), by financing publication of the book.

The Farquharson family who were the landlords of the farm Bridgend of Bush, which John Brown's father rented, had been in the district for a mere 200 years. Therefore they were newcomers to Deeside in the same sense as Brown's grandfather who had moved in from Angus in 1770. This certainly does suggest a possibility that John's ancestors might have 'come out' in the '45, but there is no way of proving this since nobody has been able to show for certain that Brown's family owed clan allegiance. In the persecutions which followed Culloden the mere hint of Jacobite sympathies was imprudent, and scions of many once-famous septs went into hiding to reappear in due time with a completely new name. The common practice was to choose a negative surname, one completely lacking in Highland associations, which explains the preponderance of Blacks, Whites, Greys, and Browns in Scotland. Indeed, by 1861 the records show there were 33,820 people named Brown. It was the third most common name in Scotland.

Donald Brown married Janet Shaw, daughter of 'Captain' James Shaw of Badenoch. She bore him six sons, one of whom became the father of John Brown. In his prepared pedigree, Doctor Robertson, whom Brown detested and who, in the end, detested Brown, made much of this tenuous association with the Shaw family but since he succeeded in muddling the deeds of the father with those of his eldest son, it only helped make the issue more confused.

However, it would be wrong to assume from all this that John Brown's father was lacking in knowledge. Before marrying Margaret Leys the blacksmith's daughter, he had been a schoolmaster, and a reputed University student and author of the very first Deeside guide. It was only after his marriage that he settled down and became a farmer.

When John was five years of age, the family moved to the Bush farm, and whilst there he attended the parish school. Later, and as already mentioned, he took employment as an ostler at Colonel Farquharson's spa hotel at Cobbleton, serving the well-to-do people who came to take the waters at Pannanich. Shortly before his sixteenth birthday however, he became a pony herd and entered the service of Sir Robert Gordon who was then the tenant at Balmoral. Thus it came about that when Queen Victoria and Prince Albert took over the old castle, John Brown was already on the strength although by then 'the fascinating and goodlooking young Highlander' had come of age, and had risen to the rank of junior ghillie.

His manner, bearing, and ability seems to have impressed both the Queen and the Prince, and he was soon appointed undergroom to the Queen's carriage. He was then chosen to lead the Queen's pony, and in 1858 succeeded the consumptive John Macdonald as personal ghillie to Prince Albert. This was the appointment which brought John Brown into close contact with the Royal couple, the more so with the Queen who, writing to her daughter in 1858, could even then declare 'Brown has everything to do for me'. By the autumn of the following year his position as the *Queen's* servant was firmly established when Prince Arthur wanted to borrow his services for an expedition of his own. The Queen bluntly informed her son that such a request was out of the question since she would not know what to do without him (Brown).

After the death of Prince Albert in 1861, the inconsolable Queen began to fear she had inherited the trait of insanity from her grandfather George III, and became concerned she was losing her mind. Her first visit to Balmoral as a widow only served to heighten her distress, and she confided to the Earl of Clarendon the fact she had actually contemplated taking her own life. Many years later, in a letter to her daughter 'Vicky', she confirmed that during that woeful Spring of 1862 the thought of self destruction had indeed, been very much on her mind.

It was whilst she was at Balmoral in the following year, 1863, than an incompetent, drunk, or confused coachman succeeded in overturning the royal carriage precipitating the Queen and the Princesses Alice, and Helena, on to the hard road. Fortunately, apart from a few minor bruises and cuts, all escaped injury*, although Brown, who was on the box with the coachman, damaged his knee as he jumped clear. Nevertheless, it was he who took charge sending ahead for help, and cutting the traces. He then set the Queen upon one horse, and the Princess Alice on the other, and insisted on leading both back through the darkness 'and would not let go for fear of another accident'.

In 1864, the Queen's medical advisers, disturbed by the deteriorating state of Her Majesty's health, attended upon her at Osborne with a recommendation that she spend more time in the fresh air. In furtherance of this, and with the tacit approval of Princess Alice, it was also suggested that John Brown be brought down from Balmoral to act as the Queen's outside attendant. It is possible that Princess Alice, who had married Prince Louis of Hesse-Darmstadt, but who was still her mother's constant comfort, foresaw that the presence of John Brown on the Isle of Wight would lessen her own periods of attendance upon the Queen and allow her more time to spend with her husband.

Although he had visited the Second Exhibition in London in 1862, and had been among the servants who had travelled to Germany with the Queen in the August of that year, Brown hated travel. But having been sent for, the masculine John, who always wore a kilt, duly presented himself at Osborne in December 1864. He was then 38 years of age, and with his blue eyes, and red-gold curly hair and beard, was undeniably handsome. In some strange manner his arrival did revive the Queen's drooping spirit, maybe it was that he served as a tangible reminder of Balmoral and

---

*　*Although during her long reign the Queen's health, from time to time, gave cause for anxiety, the only time she underwent any form of surgery was at Balmoral on the 4th of September, 1871, when Lord Lister came over from Edinburgh to lance a particularly troublesome abcess. Thereafter, the surgeon, who used his newly invented carbolic spray during the operation, openly boasted he was the only person who had exercised the divine art of surgery on the sacred body of the Queen.*

*Queen Victoria
and
John Brown,
photographed
at Balmoral
in 1863.*

happy times with her 'dear, dear, Albert'. Whatever the reason, John Brown's emergence as Queen Victoria's 'most devoted servant' and confidant, can be said to date from this point onward.

Almost before the new year of 1865 had got under way, he was confirmed as The Queen's Highland Servant, and since this appointment was held directly from the Queen, he was answerable only to her. Then, when Landseer's 'imprudent' canvas — 'Her Majesty at Osborne 1866' — was put on show at the Royal Academy's Exhibition, John Brown sprang into public notice with a vengeance. Landseer's painting, a funereal rendition in predominant shades of black, showed the Queen in the grounds of Osborne House. She was seated side-saddle on a black horse, reading a despatch. The risible aspect of the picture however, was occasioned by the fact that it included John Brown. Positioned at the head of the horse, standing four square to the Queen, and appearing much in command, the black kilted John — in terms of artistic construction — dominated the grouping.

Matt Morgan, scenic designer at the Covent Garden Opera, and chief cartoonist on the *Tomahawk*, 'A Saturday Journal of Satire' edited by Arthur a'Beckett, absorbed Landseer's gloomy offering then went to work and produced a parody. This the *Tomahawk* triumphantly published with the joyous caption 'All is Black that is not Brown'.

But despite this lampoon, and words of warning from more sober minded newpapers and magazines, the Queen went ahead and instructed Landseer to make an engraving of his portrait. Her next action was to grant John Brown the courtesy distinction of 'Esquire', and in raising his salary to accord with that of a Page of the Back Stairs, she did little to alleviate rising scandal. Neither did the revelation that she had addressed a note to Lady Biddulph, wife of the Master of the Household, Sir Thomas Biddulph, asking that a hint be dropped to the Equerries not to send for Brown at all hours, since being on the go so much 'he went to bed with swollen feet and could not sleep for fatigue'. In the face of such attitudes it is no surprise that that by 1867, the Queen and her Highland Servant had become the subject for every kind of rumour.

The most common was more or less a repeat of the canard which had been prevalent in 1858, following the death of her mother the Duchess of Kent, namely that the Queen had gone mad. Now however, a new element had been added: John Brown, who was said to be her keeper. After the death of the Prince Consort, three full years went by before the Queen would make a public appearance in London. Naturally, this neurotic desire for seclusion did tend to give such stories the cloak of credence.

Then there was the Queen's deep interest in death and the hereafter[1] For instance she left behind very explicit instructions for her own funeral which, as head of the Army, she decreed must be military in nature complete with gun carriage. She also surrounded the anniversary of Prince Albert's death with so much woeful solemnity that her family came to know it as 'Mausoleum Day'. This preoccupation with death, taken in conjunction with the then fashionable vogue of spiritualism and the much talked-of levitational exploits of Daniel Dunglas Home — plus, of course, the publicity attendant upon the exposure of fake manifestations by Professor John Anderson, 'The Wizard of the North', could all have contributed to the hearsay that John Brown was a spiritualist. He was also credited with second sight, and was said to be the medium through whom Queen Victoria kept in touch with Prince Albert.

Although it would appear that no absolute confirmation has ever been forthcoming, much speculation has swirled around the proposition, and the later claim which held that Queen Victoria was first put in touch with her departed husband at a secret seance conducted at Windsor by the noted medium Robert James Lees. Likewise at another seance it is alleged that Prince Albert, through Lee's spirit control, made it known that John Brown was to be brought down from Balmoral to act as medium in place of Lees, 'who could not be spared'.

But the most startling of the rumours was that the Queen had fallen passionately in love with John Brown, and that with the Duchess of Roxburghe standing in as witness, had contracted a morganatic marriage. Reports of the 'marriage' actually appeared in a Swiss newspaper, but when these came under the review of the Queen she dismissed them with-

1. *For a reasoned survey of Queen Victoria's attitude to spiritualism, death and the hereafter, the reader is recommended to read* Victoria R.I. *by Elizabeth Pakenham, Countess of Longford, published by Weidenfeld & Nicolson.*

out comment, although the British Minister at Berne did lodge a formal complaint with the Swiss government. It was also alleged by the pamphleteer Alexander Robertson that the Queen had travelled in secret to Switzerland, and in Lausanne had given birth to Brown's child.(*) Perhaps it is strange that no one attempted to prosecute Robertson, but it would seem that opinion at that time was inclined to leave well alone, since the evils of a full discussion of such a subject in a Court of Law would be immense.

Therefore the rumours, and the jokes concerning 'Mrs Brown' continued to circulate — as did gossip concerning Brown's high-handed attitude toward other members of the Royal family. Many of these latter stories did bear the seed of truth, in as much as when a decision touched upon her own authority she did uphold the right of her servant in certain differences between the autocratic John, and members of her family. It is also known that she was very displeased with the Princess Royal over the behaviour of her daughter, Princess Charlotte, who had refused to shake hands with Brown on the grounds that her Mama had warned her 'not to be too familiar with the servants'.

But, by and large, nobody was safe from the stinging whiplash of his tongue; his blunt, off-hand mannerisms gave continual offence to high ranking Ministers; he was rude to lower dignitaries, and once, whilst in Germany with the Queen, stalked over and silenced an over-strident band by curtly commanding the leader 'Nix with the boom-boom!' But apart from the Queen, whose movements he was said to dictate and whom, at times, he treated with rough consideration, his only true friend at Balmoral was 'Sharp' the Queen's favourite Scotch collie who guarded Brown's room during his absence.

The many accusations thus levelled against the Gaelic speaking John from Crathienard, were naturally seized upon by the comic papers of the day. They were the materials from which they fashioned their satirical darts and brickbats, and as early as 1865, *Punch* had published a mock Court Circular devoted entirely to the supposed activities of John Brown at Balmoral. The *Tomahawk*, who published the parody of the Landseer portrait, as already mentioned, went even further in subsequent issues. One cartoon, entitled 'Where is Britannia?', showed an empty throne, behind which dozed the British lion. Another, and one which possibly created the greatest furore, was the drawing over a double-page spread which was captioned 'A Brown Study'. This again showed an empty throne, but now a granite-faced John Brown leans nonchalantly against one side. He is smoking a clay pipe, and the lion squats before him in the manner of a dog with its handler. The implication is abundantly clear.

But John Brown was not without courage.

Two days after the great Public Service of Thanksgiving held in St. Paul's Catherdral on the 27th of February, 1872 to acknowledge the

* *In May, 1979 a national newspaper reported on a new claim which suggests that Queen Victoria married John Brown, and that their son lived as a recluse in Paris, where he died in the mid-1950s, at the age of 90. A Buckingham Palace spokesman said, 'There is not a shred of evidence in the Windsor archives to support these allegations'—Daily Mail, Tuesday, May 22, 1979.*

recovery of the Prince of Wales from an attack of typhoid, the Queen, travelling in an open carriage, and accompanied by Prince Arthur, Prince Leopold, and the Lady Jane Churchill, was returning to Buckingham Palace after a drive around Regent's Park. They entered the Palace courtyard, and as Brown was preparing to help Lady Jane to alight, an unkempt 18 year-old named Arthur O'Connor suddenly appeared and thrusting an old flintlock pistol over the side of the carriage, threatened the Queen. When Brown rushed him, O'Connor tried to dodge around the carriage, but Brown, in his own words 'Took hold of him with one o' my hauns, and grippit him with the other by the scruff of the neck.' He continued to 'grippit' the unfortunate O'Connor until the police arrived.

Having been declared sane and fit to plead, O'Connor faced trial, and having been found guilty, was sentenced to one year's imprisonment and twenty strokes from the lash. When the Queen heard the judgement she was furious, and declared the judges had been 'too lenient'. For his part, John Brown was publicly thanked and given an inscribed, gold Devoted Service Medal, together with an annuity of £25. This, in turn, annoyed the Prince of Wales who pointed out that Prince Arthur, who had also tried to reach O'Connor but had been too slow, only received a gold pin.

Nowadays, of course, we tend to forget that Queen Victoria was subjected to more than a dozen acts of open hostility, and as she grew older she dreaded the possibility of further attacks. When she was 63 years-old a would-be assassin named Roderick Maclean (who was, of all things, a frustrated poet!) menaced her with a revolver. This incident occurred outside Windsor station on the 2nd of March, 1882. Maclean thrust his arm into the Queen's landeau, and fired off his pistol. Fortunately, he missed, and as he was steadying himself for a second shot, he was disarmed and hurled to the ground by Brown, who had jumped from his box and gone to the aid of the Queen.

There are other versions of this outrage in which Brown's role is not so heroic. In one: Superintendent George Hayes of Windsor Police is named as the man who disarmed Maclean; in another, two Eton schoolboys are said to have belaboured the Queen's assailant about the head with their umbrellas. But to do Brown justice, it is difficult to accept that he would have done nothing, despite the fact he was far from well.

The Queen's anger at the O'Connor verdict was as nothing compared to her outburst when she received the verdict of Maclean's trial. He was declared to be 'not guilty on the grounds of insanity'. This so incensed the Queen she continued to castigate her Ministers until, in 1883, an Act was quickly passed which substituted the verdict of 'guilty, but insane', and this remained statutory law until the Act was repealed in 1946.

In 1879, John Brown developed erysipelas in the face whilst in Italy with the Queen, and he was ill for two weeks. This was the only time he was absent from the Queen's side whilst in her employ. He returned to duty after his recovery, but during the rest of the stay in Italy was obliged to protect his face from the sun. To do this he wore a wide brimmed black hat which, according to Sir Henry Ponsonby, made him look for all the world 'like an English parson on holiday who is not enjoying himself'.

In March 1883, John Brown suffered a further attack of erysipelas, following a chill which he took at Windsor. He died on the 28th March, 1883, and the Queen's grief can only be paralleled to that which she displayed at the death of the Prince Consort. But here, again, as so often is the case when one tries to fathom the truth in the relationship between John Brown and Queen Victoria, there is confusion and lack of agreement in the documentation which has survived. In the Queen's own *Journal*, there is the almost unemotional entry: 'Am terribly upset by this loss which removes one who was devoted and attached to my service.' Champions of John Brown are quick to point out that, in all probability, the entry was re-framed by Princess Beatrice who, after the Queen's death, did re-edit a great deal of her mother's personal writings. Certainly, the entry does not accord with the feeling of the Court Circular of the 29th of March, 1883 (in which the Queen had undoubtedly had a hand), nor does it display the same sensibility apparent in 1849, when the Queen wrote to her uncle Leopold, King of the Belgians, praising the qualities of Brown as a foot-man, page, and *maid*, 'since he is so handy about cloaks and shawls.'

As well as the headstone for Brown's grave, the Queen commissioned a number of *memento mori*, including a life sized bronze statue from the Viennese sculptor Edgar Boehm. When finished, this was erected at the Queen's request alongside the garden cottage at Balmoral. Beneath were inscribed the following words, suggested to the Queen by Tennyson:

> *'Friend more than servant, Loyal, Truthful, Brave,*
> *Self less than Duty, even to the Grave.'*

Poor Tennyson! Just as there were people ready to interpret his words on Brown's headstone: 'that friend given you by circumstances over which you have no control' as being evidence of the Queen's spritualistic experiences, so others were ready to invest his ambiguous phrase: 'friend more than servant' with a wealth of inner meaning. But then, what was the truth? Were John Brown and the Queen lovers? Did they contract a morganatic marriage? Who can tell? Reason however, suggests that all assertions of this nature were untrue — despite the fact that more than one observer commented upon the Queen's passionate nature. From the very beginning of her reign, Victoria left no room for doubt: she was *Queen*. Straitlaced, almost to a point that went beyond reason, she had an absolute horror of being concerned in a public scandal. She never forgave her mother, the Duchess of Kent, for being discovered in a very compromising situation with an Equerry, and the involvements of the Prince of Wales caused her much distress.

Therefore, it would seem that the concern shown, and the actions under-taken by vigilanting members of her family did far more harm than good, and we can, with hindsight, now understand that the attitudes adopted, and the advice proffered by Her Majesty's Ministers was both unfortunate, and misguided.

In the March of the year following Brown's death, the Queen, pleased

31

with the success of her second published volume *More Leaves From the Journal of A Life In The Highlands*[1]— which was dedicated to My Loyal Highlanders and especially to the Memory of My Personal Attendant and Faithful Friend John Brown — felt encouraged to attempt a third publication. She announced this would take the form of a memoir covering the life of John Brown, together with extracts from his own diaries. Apart from the great consternation caused in the Royal Household, the Queen's proposal is of great interest since it does suggest that at this point Brown's diaries were still intact a year after his death.[2]

Eventually, it fell to the lot of the Dean of Windsor, the Rev. Randall Thomas Davidson, later to become Archbishop of Canterbury, to explain to the Queen the delicate issues which could arise were Her Majesty to go ahead with the publication of her proposed memoir. For his trouble the Dean was banned from the Queen's presence. She declared herself painfully affronted by his presumptuous advice. Her book *would* be published, and she demanded of the Dean a complete apology. But this the Dean was not prepared to do, at least not in the manner dictated by the Queen. Then, just as suddenly as it started, the whole matter was dropped. Without any further reference the Rev. Davidson was restored to favour, and nothing more was heard of the proposed memoir.

Nevertheless, the question still remains: what was in the Queen's proposed book which caused so much heartsearching among those who advised her? All who saw some of the early draft have remained silent as to its content. If however, as A. A. Thomson suggested,[3] John Brown was similar in stature to the autocratic Caleb Balderstone, the aged servant of the Master of Ravenswood, or was basically at one with Tom Purdie, the faithful poacher-turned-servant whom Sir Walter Scott regarded as his 'humble and sincere friend', then his role was akin to that of the Court Jesters of Tudor and Stuart times who, as Tom Cullen points out,[4] 'pained the devil with the truth'. And so, if all the Queen intended was a cosy record of travels and pleasantly remembered 'expeditions' in the company of her privileged servant, and had intended to use John Brown's own diaries to provide a contrasting version of these same events, wherein lay the folly? Why suppress the memoir? Why burn the diaries?

In the final analysis we are left with the age-old Sophism: is the truth what we believe to be the truth? Or is it what we can prove to be right? As far as John Brown and Queen Victoria are concerned, perhaps one day the mists will lift? One hopes so; as much to justify the memory of Queen Victoria, as to benefit that of John Brown.

1. *Punch*, **commenting on the Queen's first book** Leaves from the Journal of a Life in Highlands **declared: '. . . the trait most prominent in the Queen's book is the tea-tray.'**

2. **In this connection it was claimed a few years back that Brown's diaries still existed in the archives at Windsor and it was suggested that the only diaries which had been burned were those recording spiritualistic experiences.**

3. *Let's See the Highlands* **by A. A. Thomson, published by Herbert Jenkins Limited.**

4. *The Empress Brown* **by Tom Cullen, published by The Bodley Head.**

4

HILL AND GLEN
AND HIGHLAND MEN

'The standard on the Brae's o' Mar
Is up and streaming rarely;
The gathering pipe on Lochnagar
Is sounding lang and sairly,
The Highland men
Frae hill and glen,
In martial hue,
Wi' bonnets blue,
Wi' belted plaids
An' burnished blades,
Are coming late and early.'
—ALEXANDER LAING (1787-1857)

If the build up of the land mass is to be fully appreciated, then those people who profess to be knowledgeable in such matters insist the only possible approach to Deeside is to come up from Blairgowrie, using the motor road from the south. This follows parts of the Old Military Road and is, at heart, one of the many ancient passes through the Grampians. It starts amid the agricultural glories of the Low lands in the vicinity of the Bridge of Callay, and then climbs amid progressively wilder Highland scenery, past the Spittal of Glenshee, and into the area of the 'Devil's Elbow' which in days gone by, and in severe winters, was often snowed up until late May. Even after being improved and straightened, it was still a formidable hazard. To-day however, perhaps not one motorist in a hundred spares more than a second glance for this once notorious twin hairpin bend on a 1 in 4 gradient, since it has been completely by-passed by a brand new section of the A93 which, at the pass at Cairnwell, achieves a height of 2199 feet above sea level. This makes it the highest trunk motor road in Britain.

Beyond Cairnwell, the road descends through the picturesque splendours of Glen Clunie, and after running alongside a stretch of the Clunie Water continues over a stone bridge and into the village of Braemar passing, on the right, the house in which Robert Louis Stevenson wrote much of *Treasure Island*. A little further along, on the same side of the road as it bears away toward Balmoral, is the small, but decorative meteorological observatory set up by the Prince Consort in 1855.

Militarily, this area was once of tremendous strategic importance and became a royal stronghold many hundreds of years before Queen Victoria and Prince Albert arrived on Deeside. For example: the steeply tree-clad Creag Choinneach ('Kenneth's Crag'), carries through to the present day the name of King Kenneth II, whilst in the 14th century, for the express purpose of establishing strong control over the three great passes which, at this point, link the Highlands with the Low lands, Sir Malcolm de Drummond built Kindrochit Castle. With its stout walls, most of which were ten feet thick, it was, at one time, one of the largest keeps in Scotland, and frequently used by the King, whose standard flew from the battlements.

Unfortunately, the castle became infected with the Great Disease, and in an attempt to halt the dreaded scourge — which raged across Scotland like a forest fire — it was systematically and deliberately destroyed by artillery fire levelled by a company of gunners brought in for the purpose from Blair Atholl, in Perthshire. By the custom of the day, the unfortunate victims of the disease were buried within the rubble, and by the time John Taylor 'The Water Poet' visited the area in 1618, Kindrochit Castle was already an overgrown ruin.

However, the two settlements which grew up around the castle — Auchendryne, a traditionally Catholic community, on the left bank of the Clunie Burn, and Castleton, the predominantly Protestant district, on the other, both survived, and to all intent and purpose are the conjoined basis of the modern village of Braemar, now best known for the Highland Games held each September.

HIGHLAND GAMES —
(below)
Wrestling.

(opposite)
Putting the Shot and Turning the Bar.

It is thought the first such gathering was organised in 1064 by Malcolm Canmore Lord of Kindrochit, not necessarily as a sporting occasion, but rather as an acceptable method of toning up the somewhat slack bearing and discipline of his troops. Rewards for the most proficient meant increased status in his army, thus the youngest son of McGregor of Ballochbuie who won the first ever race to the top of Creag Choinneach, was immediately appointed the King's courier.

Thereafter, such gatherings as took place were mainly spontaneous and extremely 'local' affairs arising from the seasonal hunting parties held by the nobility and gentry. Once the larders were plentifully stocked against the coming months, what more natural than they should 'let off steam' by indulging in bouts of competitive wrestling (always a popular pastime in Scotland), piping, and dancing?

In time, these impromptu gatherings began to assume a traditional aspect, and because the Scot has always held both physical strength and agility in high regard, new contests were devised to exploit these natural abilities. Men competed to see who could throw the blacksmith's fore-hammer over the greatest distance, and as a variant, the hammer was substituted by rounded stones taken from the river. The woodsmen evolved the rules and style of the essential Scottish sport of 'turning the bar', or *cabar*(*), and foot races were designed to test endurance.

The very first Scottish gathering that was completely sporting in nature, was staged at Inverey in 1554, and it was graced by the presence of Mary

*   *cabar = pole.*

34

Queen of Scots, who watched the events from beneath the prophetic 'Hangman's Tree'. Almost three hundred years later, in 1850, Queen Victoria attended a Highland Gathering at the Castle of Braemar. Included in that day's sport was the customary race to the top of Creag Choinneach, 1764 feet above sea level, which was won by Duncan, the Queen's ghillie, in the remarkable time of six and a half minutes. But this punishing performance caused permanent damage to Duncan's lungs and heart, and so grieved the Queen that, at her request, the race was never included in subsequent programmes.

But although the Queen had set her royal seal of approval on the Games, her Hanovarian ancestors considered they constituted too great an outward show of Clan, or sept allegiance, and to suppress such inherent loyalties of kinship, had the Games outlawed. They also passed an Act of Parliament prohibiting all Scotsmen from wearing or putting on 'the clothes called Highland clothes on any pretext whatsoever'. Penalties for disobeying the Act ranged from long terms of imprisonment, to transportation.

The Act of 1747 was eventually repealed in 1782, the year after a Highland Gathering had been held at Falkirk without causing any trouble. Other meetings quickly followed, but it was not until 1816 that the Braemar Wright's Society, a guild formed by the 'organised' carpenters of Auchendryne, and under the patronage of William Farquharson of Monaltrie, held their first meeting. When, in 1826, the guild re-styled its title and became The Braemar Highland Society, it also made many changes in the flavour of the Games. These changes were principally to accommodate the interest shown in their activities by the new landowners from England, although one new rule did make it obligatory for all participants in the Games to wear Highland dress. The Society received the patronage of Queen Victoria in 1848, and it is their proud boast that they have been so honoured by every succeeding monarch.

When women began to enter for certain of the contests, they too favoured the kilt, an affectation which outraged the Male Chauvinist Pigs of the day who were aghast at the sheer effrontery of women appearing in the *masculine* kilt, and appalled at the idea of them performing *men's* dances. The Aboyne Games Committee, the acknowledged arbiters on all matters concerning conduct and procedure at Highland Games, met to consider the matter. They came up with a solution on both counts by designing the Aboyne dress for women, and creating special choreography for the women's dances. Both still feature in the Games, although the Aboyne dress, with its close fitting bodice and wide, swirling skirt has been modified since its introduction.

Reverting to the *feile-beag*, or little kilt, for many generations the butt of Sassenach jokes. It is, indeed, a truly *masculine* Scottish garment, yet it was the inspiration of one Englishman, who had the assistance of another.

Thomas Rawlinson who was born in 1689 at Graythwaite in Westmorland was, at first, a Quaker, but at the age of ten years he conformed to the Church of England in accordance with the wishes expressed in the Will of his great-uncle from whom he inherited the wealthy Whittington Hall

35

estate. When he was 38, he took advantage of the commercial opportunities being opened up in certain areas of Scotland by entering into a 31 year agreement with John MacDonell of Glengarry to 'trade in the business of Pigg and other Iron' along the well wooded areas of Glen Garry.

But although he established his Scottish foundry on a community basis, he encountered many difficulties, not the least being the dress of his employees. He found that whilst the *breachan-feile* (plaid) — the ancient Highland dress favoured by most of his Highland workers — was eminently suitable for outdoor life, it was a cumbersome garment to work in, especially in a foundry. Twelve ells in length and belted to the waist, it covered the upper and lower parts of the body. But since it was the Highlander's *only* garment it could not be removed by the men when they were working because underneath the plaid they were completely naked.

It has been suggested by writers and researchers into Scottish customs and costume that the wearing of the plaid in this fashion, belted at the waist, arose from practical reasons. Such webs of cloth, being hard to come by, would have been one of a man's most valuable possessions and therefore, with true Scots providence it was used to full purpose as a garment by day, and a sleeping cloak by night.

Rawlinson also had problems with Invergarry Castle, the MacDonell's fortified tower house on the shores of Loch Oich. This had been burned by Government troops in 1720, and it was part of the tenancy agreement that he would restore the castle for his own use. Glengarry's men however, had other ideas. So strongly did they resent their chieftain's house being occupied by an Englishman, they tried to murder the unfortunate ironmaster. It is not surprising therefore, that Rawlinson maintained a close relationship with the military, and drew his friends from the personnel at the barracks, one of whom was Private Parkinson, also an Englishman, and the regimental tailor.

SOLDIER OF THE HIGHLAND REGIMENT, 1743.

It was to Parkinson that Rawlinson confided his idea of dividing the plaid into two units,[1] one part to be in the form of a cloak to cover the upper parts of the body, the other portion to be pleated, as before, but attached to a belt. Parkinson went along with the suggestion and made up an outfit to his friend's measurements, and this Rawlinson wore with great convenience 'and in the neatest manner possible'. MacDonell also saw and approved, and had his own little kilt made up,[2] but the workers at the foundry were mostly uncultured and therefore lacked the needle skills necessary to produce a fashioned garment. That being so, their costumes were ordered in bulk from Parkinson, who did the work at Fort William. Soon after, the officers at the Fort took up the Sassenach's design, and then recommended its adoption as the official dress of the Highland regiments. However, it was not until Queen Victoria observed how the harsh combed

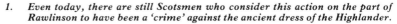
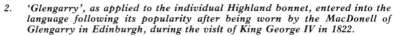

1.   *Even today, there are still Scotsmen who consider this action on the part of Rawlinson to have been a 'crime' against the ancient dress of the Highlander.*

2.   *'Glengarry', as applied to the individual Highland bonnet, entered into the language following its popularity after being worn by the MacDonell of Glengarry in Edinburgh, during the visit of King George IV in 1822.*

woollen material cut and lacerated the soldiers' knees that the order was given for softer, carded wool to be used in the weaving of the tartans for the regimental kilts. It was also Queen Victoria who suggested the kilt 'pin', this following the sight of a parading soldier on a windy day whose kilt had blown over his head. The 'pin', of course, is not functional in the accepted sense. It is merely a decorative weight to keep the kilt down.

Unfortunately, despite the bright hopes which he enjoyed at the outset of his venture, Rawlinson's foundry was a dismal failure, and after battling for seven years against tremendous odds his accumulated losses amounted to well over £7000. Saddened and disillusioned, he returned to England in 1736, and died in the following year.

During the 16th and 17th centuries, when the Forbes, Gordon and Farquharson families feuded with each other, and with the Earls of Mar, the province of Mar acquired a somewhat bloodthirsty reputation. It was as a bastion against his troublesome and unruly neighbours that, in 1628, John Erskine, to whom Mary Queen of Scots had returned the estranged estates of the Earl of Mar, commissioned the building of Braemar Castle, 'a great body of a house, a jam, and a staircase'.

Much later, following the accession of George I, the then Earl of Mar, who was known variously as 'Bobbin' Jock' or 'Bobbing John', and who had been stripped of his high Office as Secretary of State, instigated the 1715 rising. At his behest, and disguised as a hunting party, all the disaffected Jacobites met together in the Farquharson house at Invercauld. Among those present was Rob Roy, the 'Robin Hood of Scotland', in real life 'Red' Robert MacGregor, whose family had been outlawed by James VI.(*) From this conclave flowered the rising which began on the 6th of September, 1715 when the standard of King James the Eighth was raised in Braemar on a spot now occupied by the Invercauld Arms hotel. But the occasion was marred by a small incident; as the flag was unfurled, the gilt ball at the top of the flagpole fell off and crashed to the ground. This was regarded by many superstitious Highlanders as a sign that the cause would fail. Nevertheless, the *croishtarich* — a stake of wood, one end of which had been dipped in animal's blood, and the other end burned to symbolise sword and fire — was carried through the valleys and glens with all possible speed over pre-fixed routes, rallying the clans. Each eligible man who answered the call took with him his sword and firearms, and a bag containing freshly baked bannocks, and a pair of newly mended shoes, and it was a point of honour in every household that such a bag, with its contents, should be ready at all times.

But the whole project was ill considered and badly planned. Marching southwards at the head of the Jacobite army the Earl was intercepted by inferior Royalist forces under the command of the Duke of Argyll. The ensuing battle, which took place on the 12th of November, 1715 on the

---

* *The Records of Invercauld* **list the following as being present: The Marquis of Tullibardine, the Marquis of Huntly, the Earl of Breadalbane, Lords Southesk, Stormont, Drummond and Ogilvy, Lord Seaforth, the Lords Nithdale and Traquhair, the Viscounts Kilsyth, Kenmure, and Kingston, and the Lords Rollo, Duffus, Strathallan, and Nairn, and the Lairds of Auchterhouse and Auldbar, together with twenty-six Highland chiefs.**

bare uplands of Sheriffmuir, was indecisive. But many of the Earl's followers deserted, and he retreated on Perth, and the road to the Forth was closed. On the 22nd of December, 1715, the sad looking, slow speaking 'Pretender' landed at Peterhead, moved on to Stonehaven, and then to Fetteresso Castle where, on the 2nd of January, 1716 he was proclaimed James the Eighth of Scotland. 'If you are willing to die like a Prince,' declared the clansmen, 'then there are ten thousand Scotsmen willing to die for you.' But James Stuart, son of James the Second and Mary of Modena, was not of this mettle, and within a few short weeks he, and the Earl of Mar, fled in secret down the coast to Montrose and from there took ship to Avignon, in France. Their still loyal, but unfortunate supporters were left to fend for themselves, but prodded by Argyll's advancing troops fell back on Badenoch, and there dispersed.

James subsequently retired to Rome, but thirty years after the abortive rising of 1715, his son Charles Edward, the 'Young' Pretender, came to England to lead a new rebellion. He landed at Eriskay in the Western Isles on the 23rd of July, 1745, and then moved up Loch Shiel to Glenfinnan, where his standard was raised on the 19th of August, 1745. Later, he was proclaimed King from the steps of the old Tolbooth at Stonehaven, and when the Hanovarian Government offered a reward of £30,000 for the capture of 'Bonnie Prince Charlie', he replied by offering the same reward for the capture of George II. At first all went well; success followed success. By September 17th he was in Edinburgh, and four days later he defeated Sir John Cope at the battle of Prestonpans. From then on the road south was wide open and when he and his army reached Derby on December 4th it seemed as if nothing could stop their march on London. But with success almost within their grasp, his commanders, worried that so few English Jacobites had joined their cause since crossing the border, felt it was better policy to return to Scotland. Reluctantly the Prince agreed, and the northward retreat began. Four months later, on the 16th of April, 1746, his cause died, along with many loyal Scotsmen on the bloody field of Culloden.

'BONNIE PRINCE CHARLIE'
Based on the miniature by Antonio David (1732).

In the weeks that followed, Prince Charles, still with a price on his head, was intensively pursued by Hanovarian forces from Inverness to the islands of the Outer Hebrides, and then back again across the Isle of Skye. But never was he betrayed, and eventually after being hidden, disguised, guided and befriended by Scotsmen of every class, he was put aboard the French ship L'Heureux and sailed from Loch nam Uamh, near Arisaig, on the 20th of September, 1746. Twenty-one days later he stepped ashore at Roscoff in Brittany.

Farquhar, who founded the Clann Fhearchan, came to the land of Mar in the 14th century. He was the son of John Shaw of Rothiemurchus on Speyside, and one of his own children, Donald, became the owner of the Invercauld lands through marriage to the daughter of Duncan Stewart of Mar. One of their sons, the legendary Fionnlagh Mor ('Big Findlay'), a giant of a man, carried the Royal Standard at the battle of Pinkie in 1547.

But undoubtedly the most colourful member of the clan was the

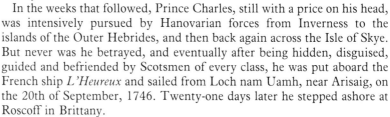

38

boisterous John Farquharson a tall, dark, free-and-easy romantic, who rode with Graham of Claverhouse against the Covenanters in 1679, and fought at Drumclog and Bothwell Bridge. In 1689 he again roused the men of Mar in support of Claverhouse (who, by then, had become Viscount Dundee) and James II, against William of Orange. He was made a Colonel, and it is as the 'Black Colonel' that he is perhaps better known through the stories which are still told of his devil-may-care bravery, his roistering love-life, and his many hair's breadth escapes from capture. All these stories are in keeping with his wild, unruly character, for this was the man who summoned servants to his table by firing off a pistol at a hanging shield, which rang like a bell; and the same, who with inferior forces hoodwinked a strong force of King' William's troops sent to capture him.

Coming upon his enemies at first light, he burst down upon their encampment within the grounds of Braemar Castle from the slopes of Creag Choinneach encouraging his men to make as much noise as possible by shouting and loosing off their firearms. The reverberating echoes led the King's troops to believe they were being attacked by a larger, and superior force. They panicked, and were routed. At the Colonel's order all the dead were thrown into the Dee, and the prisoners sent back to Aberdeen with a derisory message. Then, and to make absolutely certain there would be no further occupation by the military, he gutted the castle by fire.

He died in 1700, and found his final resting place in the ancient burial ground at Inverey, alongside his last love Annie Bann who had sustained him and shared his hide-out in Glen Ey(*) when he was being chased by General Cunningham's troops after the battle of Killiecrankie in July 1689. Although this was a Royalist victory 'Bonnie Dundee' was killed during the action, and the advantages gained were never consolidated. No stones are left to mark the graves of the Colonel and his 'lady', but it is still possible to trace the site of the burial ground a short distance NW from the Colonel's own ruined castle at Inverey.

The Farquharsons became Lairds of Inverey after Lamont of Inverey had been hung for sheep stealing, allegedly being convicted upon accusations falsely compounded by the Farquharsons. At the time of the execution, Lamont's widowed mother placed a curse upon the Farquharson family; a curse said to have been fulfilled when the tenth Laird died in 1805 and the male line became extinct. Because of this, James Ross of Balnagowan, who had married Catherine Farquharson, the sole survivor of the Laird's eleven children, eventually adopted his wife's name to ensure continuance of the family line.

Invercauld House, the home of the clan chief, stands about a mile from Braemar Castle (which is also owned by the Farquharsons), and some four miles from the village of Braemar. It is a fine, compact mansion house in the Scottish baronial style with upsurging bartisan turrets, lording chimneys, and a sturdy battlemented tower. Thomas Pennant the naturalist, who visited Invercauld in the 18th century, was much impressed by the game which then abounded in the district. He noted grouse, ptarmigans, plovers, whimbrels, snow buntings, eagles, and peregrine falcons swarming on the surrounding hills, and that both dotterels and goshawks were known to nest in the district. Grouse and ptarmigan, of course, are still very much in evidence; in fact, all the specie mentioned by Pennant continue to be recorded since the 60 to 80 breeding pairs of dotterels on the Cairngorm summits provide local sightings. The lovely little snow bunting however, is now one of our rarest breeding birds with probably no more than five such pairs in the whole of the country at any one time, and the splendid goshawk features only as a rare winter migrant. Tragically, in 1962, almost the whole of the peregrine falcon population was wiped out as a direct result of crop spraying poisons, which they absorbed from their prey, although quite recent surveys do tend to indicate a marked increase in the numbers of these spectacular birds.

Down from Invercauld House, and alongside the main A93 road beneath the towering Creag Clunie cliff, stands the 'Muckle Stane o' Clunie', a huge boulder which must have fallen from the heights above. At one time it served as a marker for the boundary separating the lands of Farquharson of Invercauld from those of Erskine of Clunie. In an almost inaccessible cave-like recess about a third of the way up the cliff itself, John Farquharson concealed the family charter during the 1715 rising. It is also said that he himself took refuge there to escape from his enemies, and

---

*   *Known as 'The Colonel's Bed', the ledge of rock is marked on local maps, and is easily accessible although care should be exercised when walking above the gorge.*

exiled on this lofty perch for nigh on twelve months he was driven near to frenzy as, night after night, he heard Government soldiers making merry in his own home below; the home in which, but a short time previously, he had acted as host to the gathering of conspiring Jacobite chieftains.

A short distance further on, the road crosses the Dee by way of the Invercauld Bridge which cost £5,000 to build. It is constructed from stone taken from Creag Clunie, and was erected to the order of Prince Albert at his own expense when he closed the old Ballochbuie road which, together with the Old Bridge of Dee formed part of the south Deeside turnpike. The Old Bridge, now on the Royal estate, and about 150 yards downstream from the new bridge, was constructed after the death of General Wade but built to his survey and was intended as a link in the Military Road. There is a Deeside legend attached to the building of the bridge which relates how, many years ago, the Seer of Glen Lui foretold that a thorn bush would grow from a pool of the Dee beneath Creag Clunie. At the time this prediction was made it was felt it could only be achieved by Divine intervention. However, shortly after the work of erecting the bridge was completed in 1752, it was noticed that a thorn tree had begun to flourish from beneath one of the arches. In this manner the Seer's prophecy was fulfilled.

The setting for the Old Bridge is certainly picturesque. It thrusts its way across the Dee at a point where the river bends and tumbles over rocky pools. Viewed against the lofty Lion's Face rock, it is easy to understand why it has become one of Deeside's most photographed bridges. On certain days the bridge is opened to allow those who wish, to visit the Falls of Garbh Allt. There are three in all, and although of no great height are thickly overhung by numerous pine and birch trees making them, for many, the most beautiful and romantic of the Deeside cascades.

Above the Falls two burns unite — the Feindallacher and the Allt Lochan an Eun, to form Garbh Allt. Between them, and running up the slopes of Lochnager, is the old smuggler's route to Glen Doll and Glen Clova. Known as the 'Smuggler's Shank', the pass over which many a tub of illicit whisky travelled on its journey from Deeside through to the south.

Back on the A93, and over the Invercauld Bridge the road runs through the afforestation areas of the Ballochbuie forest and the Muir of Inver, past the burnt out shell of the old Inver Inn, once a favourite starting point for those planning to scale the heights of Beinn A'Bhuird and Ben Avon. About a mile beyond the hotel, on a rocky hill laying toward the river, and ringed around with larch trees, is *Carn-na-Cuimhne*, the 'Cairn of Remembrance' which is the rallying point of the Farquharsons, and which tradition dates from the time when every member of the Clan called to battle would bring with him a stone to be lain down at this place. Those who survived the battle returned and took away their stones. The remaining stones were then counted, and the tally answered to the number who had died, or were missing. *Carn-na-Cuimhne* thus became the watchword of the Clan, and wherever the cry rang out, it was enough to rally the support of every clansman within hearing.

It is at this point the road begins its long curve toward Crathie.

5

THE LAIRD AND HIS LADY

*'Every year my heart becomes
more fixed in this
dear Paradise . . .'*
—QUEEN VICTORIA (1819-1901)

The announcement made in June, 1842 that Queen Victoria and Prince Albert would be spending their forthcoming autumn holiday in Scotland, excited a great deal of interest on both sides of the border since, at that time, no reigning British monarch had visited Scotland since Charles the First — except for the two mad weeks in 1822 when 'the tartan and the bagpipe being the order of the day', the 60 year-old George IV had 'capered around Edinburgh in a kilt' in the company of the Lord Mayor of London, Sir William Curtis, who was a sea biscuit manufacturer from Wapping.

George's visit had been carefully orchestrated by Sir Walter Scott, whose insistence upon the long forgotten fashion of wearing Highland dress had encouraged the clan chiefs and their followers to wear their most splendid accoutrements and regalia. To modern eyes the end result may appear somewhat over indulgent and, at times, bizarre, but the event did serve to expedite the restoration of many peerages which had been forefeit following the 1715 rising, and the '45 rebellion. It also established the ancient Highland dress as the hereditary costume of Scotland.

*GEORGE IV
Sketch based
on a lampoon
published
in 1822.*

Scott, who boarded the royal yacht when it arrived in the Leith Roads, was toasted by the King, with whisky, and the novelist, greatly daring, asked if he might keep his glass as a treasured memento. When told that he could, he carefully wrapped it and placed it in the pocket of his tail coat. Returning to his home in Castle Street, after visiting the King, he found an unexpected visitor awaiting his arrival. The naturally hospitable Sir Walter, after welcoming his guest and without thinking, sat down beside him — and upon his precious souvenir, which was shattered beyond repair.

When Queen Victoria and her husband, together with the royal party, set sail for Scotland in the late August of 1842, they did so in the *Royal George*, the same yacht as had been used by George IV. But the passage from Woolwich was slow and they were a day late in reaching Granton in the Firth of Forth. There was however, consolation in the fact that their arrival now coincided with St. Giles's day, which greatly pleased the Scots. Unfortunately, as it was very early in the morning when the royal yacht dropped anchor, most of the good citizens of Edinburgh were asleep. It was also raining heavily, so few people were about. True, they had turned out in their hundreds on the previous day to welcome the royal couple but,

The Royal George *in sight of Edinburgh, September, 1842. From a watercolour by J. W. Carmichael.*

somewhat disappointed, had returned to their homes at nightfall convinced the Queen and her husband would not consider coming ashore until around noon. How wrong they were, and how little they knew their Queen for although pregnant with her third child the 23 year-old Victoria had no intention of remaining aboard the *Royal George* for a moment longer than was absolutely necessary. She was ready, and she was going; and so it was on that wet and miserable first day in September that the Lord Provost of Edinburgh and other startled City dignitaries found themselves literally summoned from their beds to receive the Queen and her husband when they stepped ashore.

After the civic reception, Queen Victoria and Prince Albert made a brief tour of Edinburgh before, in the most appalling weather, they set off to spend their first night on Scottish soil at Dalkeith Palace, as guests of the Duke and Duchess of Buccleuch who held the palace on the understanding that the sovereign could command it as a royal residence — as, indeed, George IV had done in 1822.

The royal couple spent the next four days sightseeing. They attended a great encampment of Atholl clansmen at Dunkeld, and when visiting Dalhousie the Queen was impressed when she was told by Lord Dalhousie, who received them, that she was the first British sovereign to set foot in Dalhousie Castle since Henry IV in 1400. Further visits were made to Edinburgh, after which Prince Albert wrote home to his family in Coburg extolling the 'fairy like view' of Edinburgh from the Leith road. He also thought the people around Dalkeith looked very German, especially the old women in the mutch caps.

On the fifth day they left Dalkeith, and crossing the Firth at Queensferry, made their way to Scone (pronounced Skoon), once the Pictish capital and a town of great antiquity where all the Kings of Scotland from Malcolm IV to John Baliol had been crowned upon the ancient Stone of Scone, or Stone of Destiny. Legend has it the Stone is the 'pillow' used by

Jacob at Luz, called Bethel.[*] After travelling from Syria to Egypt, it was moved — on the advice of Moses — to Spain by Gathelus, whose son took it with him when he invaded Ireland, where it remained until shipped to Iona in the 5th century by Fergus of Dalriada. It was taken next to Dunstaffnage, which became its home for many years until Kenneth MacAlpine, who united the Kingdom of Picts and Scots in AD 843, transferred the Stone to Scone, where it rested until, in 1296, it was seized by Edward I ('The Scourge of Scotland') and carried off to London. It was placed in Westminster Abbey in a specially made chair which, since that time, has been used as a Coronation Throne.

Over the centuries however, the Stone lost a great deal of its awesome appeal, and as Addison reveals when his friend Sir Roger de Coverley visited the Abbey, it was then the practice of the guides to allow any Tom, Dick, or Harry to occupy the chair provided they 'dropped' the necessary gratuity. This antique stone carries with it the prophecy:

> *Unless the fates are faithless grown*
> *And prophet's voice be vain;*
> *Where'er is found this stone*
> *The Scottish race shall reign.*

Not so very long ago the Stone was 'kidnapped' and held in secret for some considerable time before it was surrendered on the High Altar of the Abbey of Arbroath.

They stayed overnight at Scone Palace as guests of the Earl of Mansfield, and next day drove off in procession for Taymouth Castle where their new host, the Marquess of Breadalbane, had allocated for their use the whole of the then newly completed west wing of the lavishly appointed and ornately decorated castle. In addition, and despite the short nature of the Queen's visit, the Marquess (who was responsible for re-introducing the capercaillie bird into Scotland) had even gone to the trouble and expense of enlarging the supposedly prehistoric Spey Island on Loch Tay by building on more stone, and planting out additional trees.

It was about a quarter to six in the evening when the Queen and the Prince arrived at the castle gates, where a great crowd had assembled, and where the Marquess, wearing the full dress and regalia of a Highland chieftain, stood at the head of a guard of honour drawn from Lord Breadalbane's own Highlanders, wearing Campbell tartans, Sir Neil Menzie's Royal Highland Perthshire Local Militia, in the Menzie's red and white tartan, and pipers from the 92nd Highlanders. As a spectacle it overwhelmed the young Queen. In an excited voice she cried aloud: 'Oh, my Lord Keeper! What a great quantity of Highlandmen you have got!' At this, according to a contemporary report, a mighty cheer arose from the people, and there was a great firing off of guns, and much skirling of pipes.

Later that same night huge bonfires were lit on the surrounding hills, and the ecstatic townsfolk, in true carnival mood, formed a torchlight procession which wound its way through the town and back to the castle. By then, the castle railings had been festooned with gaily coloured fairy

*   *Genesis ch. 28, vs. 16, et. seq.*

lanterns, and after a magnificent display of fireworks, a spectacular set-piece was lit, which spelled out on the lawns a sparkling message of loyalty and welcome.

From Taymouth, which marked the most northerly point of their journey, the Queen and the Prince moved on to the town of Crieff, originally called Drummond, and largely repaired and rehabilitated from 1731 onwards by James Drummond, Third Earl of Perth after it had been burned to the ground by the Jacobites in January 1716. It was whilst they were at Drummond Castle as the guests of Lord and Lady Willoughby, that Prince Albert was initiated into the 'curiously new field sport' of deer-stalking, then rapidly gaining favour as the manufacture of sporting guns became increasingly more accurate.

But so eager were the Scots to see Queen Victoria and her husband, that their intended 'holiday' rapidly assumed the proportions of a full state visit which meant that visits to the Roman site at Ardoch, and to Stirling Castle (where the Queen gave her name to a look-out on the ramparts), and to Falkirk, were sandwiched into the schedule of the single day allotted to cover the exhausting 65 mile journey from Crieff back to Dalkeith. But there was no complaint from either the Queen or Prince Albert; they were enraptured with Scotland. They loved its beauty, its colourful romanticism, its remote grandeur, and its impressive solitude. Above all else, they were charmed by the simple dignity and bearing of the people whose devotion 'evinced in every quarter and by all ranks' left an ever glowing impression upon their minds which remained with them for the rest of their lives.

From a political viewpoint the trip had also been an unprecedented success, and as the Queen and the Prince steamed homeward aboard the General Steam Navigation Company's yacht *Trident*, they could well reflect that despite the gloomy predictions of the Dismal Jimmies, there had been no unpleasant incidents, no Chartist riots, no untoward demonstrations, and no attempts made on the Queen's life.

Naturally, once safely back at Windsor, the royal couple set about the task of establishing a home of their own in the Highlands — although, at this stage, Balmoral never entered into their speculations. In 1848 they spent a three week holiday in Scotland at Blair Castle, the home of the Duke of Atholl, and which had once sheltered the Bonnie Prince, but the choice of a royal residence seemed to favour Ardverikie, the comfortable house, or lodge, which Lord Abercorn had built in 1840 on the southern bank of Loch Laggan, in Inverness-shire. Cluny Castle, home of Cluny MacPherson, Chief of the Clan Chattan was also thought to have been a possibility, but it was to inspect the house at Laggan that the Queen and the Prince, together with their family, went again to Scotland in 1847, and it could be argued that if that year had not turned out to be one of the wettest summers experienced within living memory in the Western Highlands, Ardverikie might well have become the Queen's Highland home, and a tourist target in the years to come.

As previously, the Queen and her family undertook to make the journey to Scotland by sea, travelling aboard the royal yacht, and if this preference for seaborne journeys seems strange, remember that living conditions at that time, even in the best regulated of households, were far from satisfactory. The stench from the River Thames, for example, was so abominable and far reaching that, at one stage, Parliament was seriously considering moving the House to Hampton Court. A sea voyage was therefore not only convenient, with all that good, clean, fresh air, it was a benefit to one's health.

The northward cruise, in good weather, was pleasant and enjoyable, and the family was able to make a visit to the Holy Island of Iona where, in the 6th century, St. Columba had landed and established the religious foundation from which began the Christian conversion of Scotland. They also visited Staffa, in the Inner Hebrides, which from all accounts was a jolly outing, and the Queen recorded in her diary with delightful naivety '. . . that for the first time . . . a Queen of Great Britain with her husband and children . . . entered Fingal's Cave'.

When the yacht arrived at Fort William, they all disembarked and set out to complete the final stage of the journey to Loch Laggan by carriage, but whilst driving through the famous Glencoe Pass the fine weather, which had held for so long, suddenly broke and conditions worsened with alarming rapidity. The clouds came right down, it became very cold and damp and a biting wind blew up bringing with it heavy, blinding rain. By the time they reached Ardverikie most of them were soaked to the skin, and in general they presented a wretchedly woebegone appearance.

Thereafter the rain continued almost without ceasing, day in, and day out throughout the whole of their four week stay. But notwithstanding the weather, they were able to put in an appearance at a programme of Highland games which were staged in honour of Prince Albert's birthday, and they made several short trips from the house which enabled the impressionable Albert to remark that, although wetly miserable, the area around Loch Laggan was reminiscent of Thuringen. Since then, of course, a great many changes have been wrought in the locality, principally as the result of work carried out in connection with the 1931-1943 Lochaber Power Scheme, and the construction of the great Loch Laggan dam across Glen Spean. This complex piece of hydro-electric engineering is 160 feet high and has a series of tunnels which, in turn, connect Loch Laggan to Loch Treig, and pumps the water to Fort William. The building of this dam not only increased the depth of water in Loch Laggan, it added almost five miles to its overall length.

From time to time the Prince was able to escape from the saturated environs of Ardverikie when he left to fulfil long standing public engagements at Inverness and elsewhere. But the Queen, being not so fortunate, was obliged to remain in the house by the Loch with its miserably moist prospect. At times it was so cold that writing was almost impossible. However, these drawbacks in no way lessened her deep and abiding love for Scotland, and whereas others might well have thrown aside their rose-tinted spectacles in disgust and sought forceful, explosive words with which to describe their feelings, the Queen mildly records in her *Journal*:

'. . . the weather . . . most dreadful'.

Unfortunately, worse was to follow. The journey home, also by sea, developed into a nightmare voyage, and the old proverb about it never rains but it pours, proved to be most apt. From the very moment they set sail they were beset by persistent rain and heavy squalls. Clawing their way down Kilbrannan Sound, seeking safe harbourage at Campbeltown, they were tormented by strong winds, heavy seas and, of course, torrential rain. At Campbeltown it was decided to make a run for Loch Ryan in the hope of meeting better weather around the Mull of Galloway. But once clear of Campbeltown they faced an added discomfort as the little ship began to roll alarmingly in the heavy seas, and the only change recorded when they reached the Mull of Galloway was that the yacht ceased rolling, and began pitching. Needless to state, when they did arrive back in London they were firmly resolved that the establishment of a royal residence at Ardverikie — or, for that matter, anywhere else in the Western Highlands of Scotland, was definitely out of the question. No matter how fine the scenery, it had little merit if it was forever blotted from view by blinding rain, or enveloped in a chilling blanket of low cloud.

As the crow flies, only a score or so miles separate Ardverikie and Balmoral, but between them stands the vast mass of the Cairngorms which breaks up the bad weather from the Western Highlands and prevents it intruding overmuch upon Deeside. In fact, the summer climate alongside Deeside can compare favourably with that of the English West Country. By a strange coincidence, at the same time as the royal family were enduring their dreadfully wet month at Loch Laggan, John, the son of the Queen's physician, Sir James Clark, had been the house guest of Sir Robert Gordon at Balmoral.(*) But there was nothing gloomy about his recollections, and he had returned to London singing the praises of Deeside, its glorious weather, and the ineffable charm of Balmoral. Naturally, Sir James retailed his son's rapturous stories of Balmoral to his Royal patient, and it could be at this point the Queen and the Prince became aware of the possibilities of the Eastern Highlands of Scotland, and of Balmoral in particular, since its owner, Sir Robert Gordon, had died suddenly in 1847 and his brother, the Earl of Aberdeen, who had inherited the property, had no wish to keep it.

The old Balmoral estate, the earliest known rent record for which is dated 1451, was originally owned by the Gordons, whose clan was founded by Sir Adam de Gordon the soldier statesman who carried to the Pope the declaration of liberty, asserting the Independence of Scotland, drawn up and signed by the Scottish barons at Arbroath in 1320. But despite their great political history, and calendar of military achievement, the Gordons were not true Heilandmen, being emigrants from Berwickshire, in the south, and descendants of Norman conquerors.

There were also some rather remarkable Gordon women. In 1670, for instance, whilst the Chief of the clan Gordon was away seeking revenge from the MacIntoshes for the burning of Auchindoun Castle, his wife, the

---

*   *Balmoral: from the Gaelic* bail *= village, and* moral *= majestic.*

Marchioness of Huntly, came face to face with the MacIntosh chieftain who had come to Huntly Castle to plead his cause. The meeting took place in the castle kitchen where, in mock submission, the MacIntosh stepped forward and placed his head upon a handy chopping block. This was too much for the Marchioness. Seeing her husband's enemy thus displaced she signalled her cook who thereupon despatched the MacIntosh chief with one swift stroke from his cleaver.

Another great character was the mother of the 5th Duke of Gordon, the original 'Cock o' the North'. Displaying the then newly designed Gordon tartan, she once raised a whole battalion of 'Gey Gordons' by crying, as she placed the King's shilling between her lips, 'Come now, my bonny lads! Who's for a soldier's life and a kiss o' the Duchess Jean?'

In 1662, through the marriage of the Gordon heiress Amee, Balmoral passed into the hands of the Farquharson family from Inverey, and who are said to have tricked the Gordons out of much of their best land. Unfortunately for the Farquharsons, one or two of the family developed a taste for high living, and having little regard for saving, the inevitable happened; in 1798 the family were obliged to sell Balmoral to pay off their debts.

The Earl of Fife — who never took up residence — bought the property as an investment, and in 1830 it was leased by the Earl's trustees to Sir Robert Gordon, one-time British Ambassador in Vienna. In this manner the wheel was brought full circle, after a lapse of over 175 years, the Gordons were back at Balmoral.

During his tenancy, Sir Robert wrought many changes. He first created a deer park, and then, in 1834 and with the help of his architect 'Tudor Johnny' Smith, began the work of conversion from which blossomed the second Balmoral. In 1839 additional living rooms and bedrooms were added, a square tower was constructed and, in the following year, the new kitchen wing was completed, along with all the other necessary domestic offices.

Whilst the Earl of Aberdeen had no inclination to live at Balmoral, he had frequently visited the old castle during his bachelor brother's lifetime, and therefore knew it well. In addition, and by virtue of his position at Court (he had, at one time, been Prime Minister), he was well aware that the Queen had been impressed by Sir James Clark's second-hand stories of Deeside. Therefore, and to strengthen his submission, he sent Queen Victoria three water colour drawings of Balmoral[1] which had been painted by James Giles, the artist in 1847 — the year of Ardverikie. However, although an excellent technician and familiar with Balmoral, James Giles could not resist the tendency to idyllise his subject. In this, of course, he was not alone. Many eminent Victorian artists — including the great Sir Edwin Landseer[2] — indulged in this not altogether unpleasing form of painting which has resulted in a legacy of appealing, but quite shameless

1. *These three paintings are still in existence. One, which was made over to King George V as a gift, is now in the Queen's art collection at Balmoral. The other two are kept at Haddo House.*

2. *Landseer was a frequent visitor. His first visit in 1850 coincided with his Knighthood. He gave drawing lessons to the Queen and her children, and drew or painted many portraits of the royal family, and their servants.*

48

distortions of the truth.

One of Giles's sketches *Balmoral from the North* could be classified as one such rendition, for he presents a veritable fairy-tale castle rising serene and transluscent against a spectrum tinted cloud. In the foreground, attended by his dog, stands the almost obligatory shepherd in bonnet and plaid ostensibly keeping watch over a wide-ranging flock of sheep.

Giles's *Balmoral from the South-east* is however, a more workmanlike offering. It is, in a sense, a good 'estate agent's picture' since it shows to great advantage the old castle's riotous display of decorated gables, battlemented towers, and capped turrets. It is therefore an important drawing because it is nearer to the truth, and more in keeping with the building which Queen Victoria saw for the first time on the 8th September, 1848.

In company with Prince Albert and their two eldest children, the Queen had driven in an open carriage all the way from Aberdeen harbour, along a route bedecked with triumphal arches of every size, shape, and material. At Aboyne they were entertained to luncheon by the Countess Gordon, after which they continued their journey and arrived at Balmoral 'at a quarter to three in the afternoon'. From the moment she saw it the Queen was captivated. Whilst the Ordnance Gazeteer was pleased to note the house 'belonged to no recognised order and displayed no unity of design', the Queen saw it as 'a pretty little castle in the Scottish style, with a picturesque tower, and a garden in the front'.

'Little' was the operative word, for the house was not large enough for full scale entertaining, nor had it been designed to accommodate the Royal Household, along with various Court officials and the retinue of servants. The diarist Greville, who visited Balmoral in 1849, agreed that whilst the house was small, it accorded with the Highland lifestyle of the Queen and the Prince who lived as gentlefolk, and without pretention. Often, he observed, Queen Victoria would walk out alone, and was not above entering some humble cottage where she would sit and enjoy a cosy chat with the womenfolk. The solitary policeman, who was the Sovereign's sole protection whilst at Balmoral, was also expected to patrol the grounds and shoo away the inquisitive, or the uninvited.

But not all shared Greville's comfortable picture, and stories of the Queen's Ladies in Waiting 'living-out' in cottages on the estate,(*) and having their meals trundled out to them on wheelbarrows, were eagerly seized upon by disputatious critics who denounced the whole set-up as being bogus and a sham. They even coined a word for what they considered to be a royal folly; they christened it 'Balmorality'. Not that these criticisms deterred Queen Victoria. She was immensely happy, and in 1852, after protracted negotiations, Prince Albert purchased both the house and the estate from the Trustees of the Earl of Fife for the sum of £31,500. The property, comprising 17,400 acres, was then made over to the Queen as a personal gift from her husband.

* *Nearly fifty years later, in 1895, the new Balmoral suffered similar shortcomings. Marie Mallet, Maid of Honour to Queen Victoria, records that when the King of Portugal visited the castle, several gentlemen of the Royal Household (who were turned out of their quarters to make room for the Portuguese suite), were obliged to live in a nearby tin cottage.*

BALMORAL, from an engraving made shortly after the building was completed.

It was about this time that the Scottish eccentric James Camden Neil died, leaving Queen Victoria an unexpected windfall of close on a quarter of a million pounds. Part of this money the Queen set aside for the redevelopment of Balmoral. This involved the demolition of the 'pretty little castle' and on the 28th of September, 1853, the foundation stone for the third, and present Balmoral, was laid. The minister from Crathie offered up blessings, and William Smith the architect, personally sealed the cavity in which had been placed a bottle containing a parchment signed by the royal family, together with a selection of the 1853 coinage.

The choice of Smith was a happy one. The son of 'Tudor Johnny' Smith, he was a man well respected in his profession, and gifted with a natural flair in the use of granite. He was also an insistent perfectionist, tolerating nothing but the very best of materials, and workmanship which was of the first class. In this he was matched by James Beaton, his equally meticulous chief mason. It is not surprising therefore, that the hand-dressed light-grey Invergelder stone which they produced for Balmoral is without peer in the whole of Scotland.

Despite the Queen's proud assertion that the new castle was 'my dearest Albert's own creation', there can be little doubt that Smith was responsible for the overall design and construction of the building. This is not to imply that the Prince had no hand whatsoever in the arrangements; far from it. Smith, like the competent craftsman he was, would have insisted upon frequent consultations with his royal client, and any suggestions made would have been considered and, where practicable, incorporated into the structure — as, for example, the series of bas-reliefs of St. George, St.

50

Andrew, and St. Hubert, on the west front. After all, the property with which he was dealing was not a State domain, but had been privately purchased and one consideration which the Prince would most certainly have impressed upon Smith would have been the fact that both he, and the Queen, did not want the new Balmoral to be another royal palace. True, the new building needed to be larger than the old castle, but it did not have to be *too* large. One can easily picture the patient Albert explaining to Smith that what was required was a Highland home *as they understood it*. A home, in fact, for the Laird and his wife — even though his 'lady' would always wear the Order of the Garter, in diamonds, when in residence.

Shortly after the foundation stone had been laid, a mysterious fire destroyed most of the completed work. But despite this set-back, and the subsequent strikes among the workmen,[1] the building progressed to such an extent that parts of the new house were ready for occupation when the royal family visited Balmoral in the following year. As usual, the Queen recorded the event in her *Journal*:

> 'At a quarter past seven o'clock we all arrived at dear Balmoral. Strange, very strange, it seemed to me to drive past, indeed *through*, the old house[2] . . . The new house looks beautiful . . . an old shoe was thrown after us into the house for good luck when we entered the hall. The house is charming; the rooms delightful; the furniture, papers, everything perfection!'[3]

The Balmoral building comprises two separate blocks with connecting wings, each with its own courtyard. At the eastern end of the south block there is a small battlemented tower capped with a canopy, whilst the large tower — which is 35 feet square — has a stone carving of the Royal Arms of Scotland on the south face, and features a clock, and a series of romantically inspired bartizan turrets. In the main, this tower is 80 feet high, with an overall height of 100 feet if one includes the small circular tower which surmounts it.

The gables of the windows between the tower and the carriage porch are decorated with gilded crests of Saxe-Coburg, with Prince Albert's own coat of arms above the principal battlemented porch on the south front. From this main entry one steps into a hall and then, in turn, through to the central corridor from which rises a staircase leading to the royal apartments on the first floor. The withdrawing room, dining room, and library are all on the ground floor.

The ballroom, the largest room in the house (it measures 68 feet by 25 feet), is nevertheless a modest affair, as indeed are most of the rooms.

1. *What Queen Victoria thought of this militant action is not known.*
2. *Portions of the old house, which still remained at that time, were used to accommodate members of the Queen's official and domestic staffs.*
3. *It is possible to gain an impression of how the new Balmoral looked to Queen Victoria by studying the painting made by the Aberdeenshire artist James Cassie, RSA, which was originally exhibited at the Royal Scottish Academy. Another picture, a water colour by Sam Bough, RSA., will also repay inspection. It now hangs in the Aberdeen Art Gallery. Incidentally, both pictures were painted before the great screen of rare conifers grew to maturity.*

When first conceived, candlelight was the order of the day, but nowadays sprig chandeliers hang down from the panelled ceiling, with clustered lights set in sconces. The large recess in one of the walls, framed by a neo-Gothic prosenium arch, is used by the band on gala occasions. The series of deep windows which pierce the opposite wall, and which are hung about with curtains of Balmoral and Royal Stewart tartans, open out on to the terrace, and the garden beyond. Entrance to the main building is through the doorway on the mezzanine landing above the twin staircase curving up from the ballroom floor.(*)

In their infatuated frenzy for all things Scottish, the Queen and Prince Albert became caught up in what has since been termed 'tartanitis'. Prominent in the rash of designs used for curtains, covers, and carpets, were the Royal Stewart and Hunting weaves, the choice of which was never considered to be at all out of place by the contradictory Queen, who was a staunch, self-confessed Jacobite, yet shunned the very name of the 'Young Chevalier'. It was after a special linoleum had been made up with a tartan pattern that the royal couple turned to creating their own tartans: the Queen designed the Victoria tartan, and Prince Albert the Balmoral, a black, red, lavender, and grey weave used exclusively by the royal family.

For many, the Highland motif was overworked. Certainly it was the opinion of Lord Clarendon, who maintained there were enough thistles in the decor of the Balmoral dining room to choke a donkey. Lord Rosebery was another who found the Balmoral dining room distasteful, describing it as the world's ugliest room — 'worse even than the one at Osborne'. The sycophantic Disraeli however, who discovered the library to be 'small, square, and very cosy', lavishly praised the creature comforts provided and the arrangements made for his entertainment, and when the gratified Queen presented him with two albums containing views of Balmoral, he acknowledged the gift by declaring that with these books beside him he would be able to live among 'your Majesty's favourite scenes'. But in truth, Balmoral was not to Disraeli's taste, and to his intimates he deplored its isolation from the seat of Government.

Among the many royal visitors to Balmoral were King Leopold II of the Belgians, whose nails were so long he could only shake hands with two fingers; King Carlos of Portugal, whose prodigious appetite was almost unbelieveable; Prince Ferdinand of Bulgaria, whose personal bodyguard slept outside his master's door, and Tsar Nicholas of Russia, who found the bewildering variety of stark-eyed stag's heads, and the great displays of dirks, daggers, claymores, and other warlike weapons with which the old Scots warriors wreaked their mayhem so overpowering, his nerve failed him and he was obliged to quit the castle and seek sanctuary in a more restful atmosphere.

But to Queen Victoria Balmoral was always her 'dear Paradise'. It was her favourite home, and in it she held sway for more than fifty years subjecting all concerned to the vagaries of her firmly held ideas about

---

*   *In 1891, The D'Oyly Carte Company staged a performance of* The Mikado *in the ballroom at Balmoral, the first of many subsequent entertainments by professional theatrical and opera companies, and virtuoso performers.*

matters of health. One such opinion was that heat was unwholesome, whilst cold was wholesome, which went rather hard on those who lacked the Queen's spartan outlook and passion for open doors and windows. Mostly it was her Ladies in Waiting who suffered, for although some of the rooms were warmed by open fires, fuel was always in short supply, causing a visitor to record in his diary that one of Her Majesty's Ladies, who sat next to him at dinner, looked 'positively blue with cold'.

But the new Balmoral made an auspicious start. Shortly after the royal party arrived for their visit in 1855 came the good news of Sebastopol, conveyed, as already recounted, by the saddle-weary station master from Banchory, and at about the same time the 23 year-old Prince William Frederick of Prussia, who was then a guest at the castle, formally approached the Queen and Prince Albert, requesting the hand of their daughter Victoria, in marriage.

Victoria and Albert were overjoyed at the prospect, but in view of the fact that the Princess Royal was then not yet fourteen years of age, and still at school, it was suggested the engagement be kept a family secret until the following Easter when the young Princess was due to be Confirmed. But, as is the way with the young in love, they tend to upset adult applecarts. The Princess and Prince William were no exception. On the 30th of September, 1855 they went riding together, and on Craig-na-Ban the Prince spied some white heather. Climbing from his saddle he picked it, and as he gave it to the Princess he 'spoke his heart' in keeping with the romantic dictates of the period. After hearing him out, the Princess Royal reached over and pressed his hand. In this manner the bargain was sealed for good and all.

Almost the first person to be informed of events was the Queen's Father Confessor, King Leopold of the Belgians, the uncle of both the Queen and Prince Albert, and a self-styled authority on all matters English. The British Cabinet were also informed, and somehow or other the 'secret' engagement became the common topic of conversation at all levels of society, with *The Times* 'thundering' its disapproval. There was also a revival of some anti-German feeling, but the engagement went ahead and was *officially* announced on the 16th of May, 1856. In the following year — on June the 25th, 1857 — Prince Albert received the Royal Patent to the title of Prince Consort, and seven months after, on the 25th of January, 1858, the young Princess, who was then in her eighteenth year was married to Prince William in the Chapel Royal of St. James's.

Having seen the star-crossed lovers riding across the heather clad slopes above Balmoral, who could have foreseen them as instruments of Fate? For within a year of their marriage, almost to the day, on the 27th of January, 1859, the Princess gave birth to a son. The first of eight children, he was christened Wilhelm, and grew up to become Kaiser Wilhelm II, the man who led his country against Britain in the 1914-1918 war.

6

THE END OF
THE BEGINNING

'I am the monarch of all I survey,
My right there is none to dispute.'
—WILLIAM COWPER (1731-1800)

When Charlotte, the Prince Regent's natural successor and only daughter died in childbirth on the 6th of November 1817, Parliament saw in her decease the need for a new, and cold-blooded re-appraisal of the overall prospects of succession.

Thus it came about that Edward, Duke of Kent, after discarding the French Countess, Julie de St. Laurent, with whom he had lived for 27 years, and whom he had morganatically married during a period of service in Nova Scotia, became the husband of Victoria Mary Louisa, widow of Emich Charles, Prince of Leiningen-Dachsburg-Hardenburg. In the following year, on the 24th of May 1819, the new Duchess of Kent gave birth to a daughter, at Kensington Palace, in London. After a great deal of vacillation upon the part of the Regent, who was required to approve the given name, the infant was christened Alexandrina Victoria. She was then fifth in the line for succession.

Within eight months of her birth, little Alexandrina lost her father, the Duke of Kent, who died at Sidmouth on the 23rd of January 1820. Then, before that same week was out, came news that her grandfather, King George III, had died at Windsor on the 29th of January 1820. Although the nominal head of the country, the old King, who had reigned for sixty years, had been hopelessly insane since 1810.

THE DUKE OF KENT, Queen Victoria's father. Based on the portrait by George Dance (1818).

Less than two decades later the Regent, who had become George IV, and his brothers Frederick Duke of York, and William Duke of Clarence, were all dead. Frederick died first, in 1827; then George IV, in 1830, and finally the Duke of Clarence who, as William IV reigned seven years. At his death on the 20th of June 1837, two messengers rode through the night to Kensington Palace. It was half past two in the morning when they arrived, and having been awakened from her sleep, the young Alexandrina came downstairs to be informed with all due deference, she was now Queen of England.

Then nineteen years old, the new Queen had, with increasing intensity, been educated to fulfil this royal rôle by her mother (whose political opinions she had absorbed from Lord Melbourne), and the Duchess of Northumberland. In her growing up she had been vivacious and independent, and although confessing to be 'rather small for a Queen', she lost no time in discarding her initial name in favour of the secondary Victoria.

54

The prospect facing the young Queen was daunting, and unenviable. Overseas respect for the British monarchy had fallen to a low ebb, and Sir Sidney Lee records the fact that many people at that time were prophesying that her Coronation would be the last seen at Westminster. The popular writer George William McArthur Roberts was one such dissident, and loudly proclaimed the grand fact 'that Monarchy is a farce, since a mere schoolgirl can be put up as the throned puppet of the Punch and Judy Show of Royalty.'

In the event, the ceremony which attended the crowning of Victoria on the 28th of June 1838, was simple in the extreme, and in the months that followed she turned with increasing regularity toward the comforting reassurances of Lord Melbourne, her great friend and counsellor. Since her Sovereignty, one factor above all others occasioned her a great deal of apprehension: the prospect of marriage. In the end, and despite her fears, it was she who proposed to Prince Albert of Saxe-Coburg-Gotha, a tiny, impoverished Duchy in Thuringia, whose ruling family Bismarck had scathingly dismissed as 'the stud farm of Europe.'

On the day of their wedding, which took place in the Chapel Royal of St. James's on the 10th of February 1840, Prince Albert became a naturalised British subject. He was also given the title of His Royal Highness, and became Consort the same year. In the 21 years she was married, Queen Victoria bore her husband nine children: Victoria (who became Empress of Germany, a match disapproved by her adoring brother Albert, who became King Edward VII); after the Prince of Wales came Alice (who married Louis IV, Prince of Hesse), then Alfred (who married Marie, daughter of Alexander II of Russia); he was followed by Helena, also known as Lenchen (who married Prince Christian of Schleswig-Holstein), and Louise (who married the Duke of Argyll); next came Arthur (who married Louise of Prussia), and Leopold (who married Helen of Waldeck and Pyrmont); finally, came the baby of the family, Beatrice, who became the wife of Prince Henry of Battenburg. Through these marriages, and those of their offspring, the influence of the Royal Family of England spread into every major nineteenth century European court.

It was these relatives who began to assemble in 1901 when, on the 17th of January it became known that the aged Queen had lost her memory. During the five days which followed she rallied sufficiently to ask for Turi, her favourite Pomeranian dog. But there was no mistaking the end was at hand, and her last word was one of recognition to her eldest son, who wept bitterly. She died at Osborne, on the Isle of Wight, at half past six on the morning of the 22nd of January 1901, and in the arms of Kaiser Wilhelm II. She was then 82 years of age, and during her long life had succeeded in elevating the prestige of the British Crown to a point never before achieved, nor ever attained since. Since no undertaker was permitted to be present at her passing, it was the Kaiser who also undertook the task of measuring her for her coffin. It was at this time that Queen Victoria's diaries passed into the possession of Princess Beatrice and she, in fulfilment of a charge laid upon her, transcribed passages from the Queen's mss. into blue copybooks, burning the original as she went. The work took many years, and it is understood that a great deal of the original writing was destroyed without being copied, a fact which greatly distressed both King George the Fifth, and Queen Mary.

The new King was nearly sixty years of age when his mother died, and she had reigned for so long — nearly 64 years, the longest of any English sovereign — that all understanding of the correct procedure for crowning a new monarch appeared to have been forgotten. So complete was the ignorance that Lord Esher was driven to make the acid comment that one would have supposed the English monarchy dead since Alfred.

When the new male heir to the Throne was born on the 9th of November 1841, at the Queen's express wish he was christened Albert Edward. By this stratagem she fondly hoped to establish Albert's name in the kingly lineage of England. She also sought to impose her wish that her son's descendants would bear the names of Albert, or Victoria.[1] Almost from the beginning however, the young Prince was known by the diminutive of 'Bertie', and when the time came, he settled all doubts and scotched his mother's plan by surprisingly and resolutely informing his Privy Council that he wished to be known by his second name: Edward. This was a name with strong Saxon roots, and one which had already been borne by six English monarchs, the last of which had been the son of Henry VIII and Jane Seymour. As a King he also righted what he considered to be one of his mother's wrongs: he accorded to the children of his daughter Louise (The Duchess of Fife), the style of Highness, which Victoria had refused.

As a boy, the Prince of Wales had been subjected to a frightening programme of education designed by his high-minded father who sought, with the Queen's approval, to create a monarch in his own image. There is no doubt that poor Bertie suffered both mentally and physically, and he carried with him to the grave the physcological scars of his early scholastic battles with a curriculum entirely beyond his intelligence and understanding. How many nine year old boys are able to comprehend the philosophies of Cicero, or the Philippics of Demosthenes? Yet this is what Albert, aided by the Baron von Stockmar, expected of his son.

Then too, there was always a protective 'guard' surrounding him at all times, and wherever he went, and he was rigidly screened against all outside contacts whilst a scholar at Edinburgh, and Oxford. But despite all this security, in 1861, whilst his son was at Cambridge, his balding father[2] was shocked to receive news that whilst serving as an officer in the Guards, at the Curragh, the heir to the Throne had been on intimate terms with an actress named Nelly Clifden.

Although in an extremely low mental state of physical health, he went to Cambridge to confront his son, in person. Three days later, returning to Windsor, Albert collapsed, and within fourteen days was dead of typhoid

1. *Edward did, in part, carry out 'Gan-Gan's' wishes by naming his first-born, Albert Victor, and his youngest daughter, Victoria. Contrarily, however, the one was always known as Prince 'Eddy', the other, as 'Toria'.*
2. *By 1860, Prince Albert had taken to wearing a wig before breakfast, as a guard against the cold.*

fever. Better informed present-day medical opinion is inclined to attribute Albert's fatal illness to the atrocious sanitary arrangements at Windsor, but at the time the Queen was in no doubt the prime cause of her beloved husband's death had been the strain of dealing with the recalcitrant behaviour of her eldest son.

In the years immediately prior to his death the perceptive Albert had devoted a great deal of time and thought to the selection of a wife for his heir. Indeed, during the interview with Bertie at Cambridge, he had stressed quite firmly to that young man that his only hope of salvation lay in an early marriage. However, the choice of a bride was rather limited, and the list of probables considerably shortened when the autocratic Queen announced it was her desire that her future daughter-in-law should be good looking, educated, intelligent, quick-witted, easy to get along with, and yet not without character or determination. On the other hand, Albert was not so materialistic. 'We are too fair,' he said. 'We need people with darker hair.' Perhaps he, above all others, realised the necessity of stabilising the rather shaky Hanovarian pedigree.

Scouts and emissaries, some openly, some surreptitiously, scoured the courts of Europe for this paragon among women; this 'brood mare.' Even the Princess Royal, who was then married, was pressed into service and despite personal misgivings about Prussia's reactions, it was she who suggested Bertie's fourth cousin, the Princess Alexandra of Schleswig-Holstein-Sonderburg-Glucksburg, daughter of the hard up Prince Christian of Denmark.

In 1862, Queen Victoria met the young Princess at Laeken Palace in Belgium, and was extremely understanding of the deafness with which Alexandra was afflicted. The loving bond affectionately forged between them lasted throughout the rest of the Queen's lifetime. At the end of the meeting at Laeken, Victoria gave Alexandra a sprig of 'lucky' white heather, which had been plucked on the hills above Balmoral. Whether she did this out of sentiment, or whether by following the pattern set by her daughter on her betrothal years earlier she sought to establish the white Scottish heather as a traditional love-token, it is difficult to say. Whatever the reason, Alexandra took the heather and showed it to Bertie when he proposed to her. The future King chose to recognise the offering as an indication of his mother's absolute approval of his bride to be.

Their marriage took place on the 10th of March 1863, in St. George's Chapel, Windsor. A chorale, composed by Prince Albert, was sung during the ceremony, and the widowed Queen 'horribly overcome', watched from Catherine of Aragon's closet. She declined to attend the wedding breakfast, but in Albert's name, as well as her own, made a gift to the newlyweds of diamonds and opals. It was as the Prince and Princess were driving away from the palace in an open landau to begin their short honeymoon at Osborne, that the lonely and rather pathetic figure of the Queen was seen standing at one of the corridor windows acknowledging their farewells.

At first Bertie and his new bride made their home in Buckingham Palace, after which they moved to Marlborough House, where they established around them their own select and compact 'set' of friends. For the most part the men were rich, cultivated, well connected, and well informed. The women were beautiful. They moved in a glittering hothouse atmosphere which spawned intrigue, and bred scandals which made household names out of such as Dilke, Aylesford, Mordaunt, and Tranby Croft.

This mode of living was far from pleasing to Queen Victoria, and when the Prince of Wales was injudicious enough to hint to his mother that she modify the adulative references to John Brown which were to appear in her proposed book *More Leaves from a Journal of Our Life in the Highlands*, she informed him, with some asperity, that she found such criticism out of place coming from one who lived in a circle in which indiscretion was the rule rather than the exception, and where there was not the slightest uprightness of principle. But the Prince came again to this subject when he received his copy of the book. This time he expressed open doubt as to whether the Queen should expose her private life to the world in this fashion, adding the barb that some comment might be forthcoming when it was noticed that never once did she mention his name.[1]

Queen Victoria's love of Balmoral, and the indelible mark she left on its early history, often obscures the fact that Edward knew the place for far longer than his mother, for he too had been a passenger in that tartan decorated coach which had conveyed the royal family from Aberdeen to Balmoral on the occasion of their very first visit in 1848. Like his mother he had seen the old castle demolished, and had seen William Smith's new building rise from the ruins. He had also been most active on nearly every one of his mother's Great Expeditions, returning to Balmoral tired and weary from physical strain and the exertion expended in keeping pace with the nimble, fleet-footed ghillies who, apart from Brown, respected his early prowess as a hillman.

It was also Edward who christened the new Balmoral 'the house of a thousand draughts', and it is not surprising one of his first acts upon taking over was to install an efficient system of heating. He also introduced modern sanitation and plumbing, and converted the private chapel on the ground floor into a billiard room.[2] In other areas however, his desires to urbanise the rusticity of 'Our Highland Home' were curbed by Alexandra.

Little love had been lost between the Prince and John Brown who, during his lifetime, had never attempted to disguise the rather poor opinion he held of his future King. Queen Victoria did not help matters. Whilst accepting her eldest son as her own caricature, she was constantly making unflattering comparisons between 'poor, chinless Bertie', and the 'splendid' Brown. Edward never forgot the smart he suffered from these humiliations, nor the fact that his mother invariably sided with Brown, against him. He did once attempt to put his foot down by refusing to go to Balmoral because, in the matter of certain grouse shooting rights, the

1. *This omission was rectified in the 3rd edition, when a description of Bertie's visit to Balmoral in 1875, was included.*
2. *At Windsor, it was John Brown's apartment which underwent similar transformation.*

H.R.H. The Prince of Wales, and Princess Alexandra. A photograph taken on their wedding day, the 10th of March 1863.

Queen had countermanded his orders in favour of Brown. This show of defiance finally petered out in the face of Victoria's displeasure, which lasted for several weeks, during which time she refused to hold any sort of communication with her son.

Even after his marriage there was no easing of the situation, and the Prince was infuriated when he learned that Brown had reported back to the Queen that the ghillies ball, given by the Prince and Princess of Wales at Abergeldie, had fallen far short of the accepted standard.

But these clashes between Bertie and Brown — whom the Prince once called 'that drunken ghillie' — were on a domestic level. The more important issues with his mother impinged upon those matters of State and Government which Edward felt the Queen could reasonably discuss with him. Instead she chose to turn to Brown, that sturdy link with her dear departed Albert, in the assumption that Brown's uncluttered mind was more capable of producing the down to earth reasoning which she found lacking in her Ministers. If, and when, Edward had the temerity to venture a political opinion to his mother this was more often than not dismissed out of hand; he was refused access to the most trivial of State papers, and was not allowed to deputise for his mother even though, as far back as 1868, it had been suggested in the *Tomahawk* that Edward should be appointed Prince Regent.

When Edward became King, John Brown had been dead for nearly eighteen years, but the royal memory was evergreen, and with all the fervour of a Crusading knight, Bertie set about erasing the imprint of John O'Crathienard from the various royal residences, including Balmoral.

Pictures and photographs were burned, portrait busts were smashed, taken down, or hidden away. The over sized and specially commissioned statue of 'The Queen's Friend More Than Servant', the work of Edgar Boehm, had turned bright green after being placed in position in the cottage garden. Thereafter to the local womenfolk, and especially during the hours of darkness, it became an object of great awe. Edward however, had no such worries, and to his orders the statue was dismantled and re-erected on a new site, well off the beaten track, in a little dell behind Baile-na-Choil, the house built by the Queen for John Brown and which, when its furnishings and appointments were viewed, gave rise to speculation as to the former ghillie's financial standing.

The fact that a great deal of Victoria's Highland home remained to her plan was due to Queen Alexandra, and her insistence that the majority of her mother-in-law's favourite treasures were to remain as *she* had placed them. It was quite an ordeal for Queen Alexandra to make her first visit to Balmoral after the old Queen's death. She dreaded entering the castle and not finding Victoria in residence, and the fact she allowed so few changes (although once or twice Edward stole a march on her), was a graceful reflection upon her understanding, since there must have been a great many alterations she would have loved to have made.

It was not until after her own husband's death, and her son had succeeded as George the Fifth, that she felt free from obligation, and in a

*FOUR
GENERATIONS.
A group
photograph
of Queen
Victoria,
together with
her son, later
King Edward VII;
her grandson,
who became
King George V,
and her great-
grandson
David, who
reigned briefly
as King
Edward VIII,
and was
later Duke
of Windsor.*

letter to her daughter-in-law (Queen Mary), she recalled the Balmoral wall-papers — in particular the 'appalling' paper in the sitting room, and 'the perfectly sickly pink moire' which graced some of the other walls. But Queen Alexandra's great gentleness is apparent in her summing up: 'poor, dear Grandmama's taste in wallpaper was rather sad, and very doubtful.'

Edward the Seventh's reign lasted barely ten years, but in view of his achievements in that short time, it constitutes as great an epoch as did his mother's, and the superior measure of 20th century regard over that of the 19th century, is reflected in the rigid classification of that which was 'Edwardian', and that which was 'Victorian'. In the end, the latter become a synonym for something, or somebody, who was musty, old fashioned, and out of date.

Prince Albert Victor, Duke of Clarence, who was always known as Prince Eddy, was the King's heir. Born prematurely, and the first of Edward and Alexandra's five children, he grew up to be mentally immature. He was however, sensual and pleasure seeking, and possessed an overpowering attraction for women, and his name has been sensa-tionally linked with the Jack the Ripper murders which took place in the east end of London in 1888.(*) In all, five girls are believed to have met their deaths at the hands of the sadistic 'Ripper' who earned his grisly soubriquet from the gruesome manner in which he disembowelled four of his victims.

When Prince Eddy died in 1892, at the age of 29 years, his brother George, and Edward's second son, became heir-apparent. He was created Prince of Wales on the 9th of November 1901, his father's sixtieth birthday.

Extensively mourned by his people, King Edward died on the 6th of May 1910, and Queen Alexandra who exhibited for her husband many of the deep mourning symptoms which had been lavishly displayed by Queen Victoria at the death of Prince Albert, took over and lavished her affection upon Caesar, the King's favourite fox terrier. The little dog, who had walked in his master's funeral cortege, behind the coffin and in charge of a Highland servant, became the Queen's constant companion, and no doubt represented for Alexandra a living contact with her dead husband.

In his Will, the King had directed that all his private and personal correspondence — especially those letters which had passed between himself and Queen Alexandra — were to be burned. Balmoral and Sandringham, the two royal houses, were left to his son George, with whom he always enjoyed a deep, loyal, and affectionate friendship.

Shortly afterward, King George the Fifth, and his wife Queen Mary, moved from Abergeldie and became the third Royal occupants of Queen Victoria's 'dear Paradise.'

---

*   *Magnus Linklater (Sunday Times — 1st November 1970); reviewing an article by Thomas Stowell, which appeared in the* Criminologist, *the journal of forensic science and criminology.*

7

THE CONTINUING STORY OF OUR LIFE IN THE HIGHLANDS

'Make a home happy and
you will be happy at home.'
—CHARLES HADDON SPURGEON (1834-1892)

As the years have rolled on since 1910, each new Sovereign tenant at Balmoral has added to the story, and left his or her own mark by adding to the comfort of the building, or the lustre and glory of the gardens.

In the latter sphere Queen Mary was most active, and was responsible for the development of the splendid sunken gardens. Both she, and her husband King George the Fifth, were excellent hosts, and revived the practice of inviting professional theatrical companies to perform at Balmoral. Also as an indication of the great changes which were then coming about through the accelerated progress in the manufacture of motor cars, and road building, King George was able to motor down from Balmoral to London on the eve of the General Strike, in 1926.

During King Edward the Eighth's short, but dramatic reign, he spent only one brief summer in the Deeside Highlands, which he loved so well. He was however, responsible for stringent economies, and arrived with only half the normal retinue. He had also sent on ahead instructions to the effect the servants were not to line the drive when he arrived, and he took over the bedroom of a major servant, who was moved to other quarters during his visit. His only party at Balmoral was when he entertained Mrs. Wallis Simpson, whom he subsequently married, and who became the Duchess of Windsor. Her contribution toward the modernisation was to introduce on to the Balmoral menus the 3-decker toasted sandwich.

As Prince of Wales, he developed a liking for bagpipe music and, in time, became a proficient performer on the instrument. However, there was one occasion, when he was staying at Balmoral following the launching of the *Queen Mary*, that his father heard him receiving tuition from the King's Piper. Throwing up the window, King George leaned out and advised his son to give up playing and leave the art to the Highlanders. But David persevered, and eventually conceived a pipe tune which he called *Majorca*, and this he played for his guests during the visit of Mrs. Simpson.

King George the Sixth, who succeeded to the Throne following the Abdication of his brother, shared his enthusiasms between Balmoral and Sandringham, although he was extremely happy in the Highlands — as,

QUEEN MARY, and George VI and Queen Elizabeth (then the Duke and Duchess of York) walking in the gardens at Balmoral in 1924.

indeed was his wife Queen Elizabeth. As a girl, she had spent much of her time at Glamis Castle, in Angus, where her second daughter, Princess Margaret, was born in 1930. Along with the present Queen, they had also enjoyed many happy family holidays at both Abergeldie, and Birkhall.

On February 6th 1952, King George the Sixth died, and his eldest daughter Elizabeth became Queen, and the new chatelaine of Balmoral. Although now more accessible, and almost 130 years old, the castle continues to be a retreat for the Royal Family; a place for relaxation (although the despatch boxes arrive with unfailing regularity), and a home which perhaps, the Queen, with her husband Prince Philip, and their children, Prince Charles, and Princess Anne, together with Prince Andrew and Prince Edward, use and enjoy to greater advantage than any since Queen Victoria. It remains a 'dear Paradise'. Long may it continue.